If you're a Student, Business Owner, Professional, or entirely new to Google Workspace or just want to get the most out of it without feeling overwhelmed, this book is for you. Written in a clear, everyday style, it takes you by the hand and walks you through each tool, step by step. No complicated jargon—just practical, real-world guidance that makes learning easy.

Whether you're a student juggling assignments, a professional managing tasks, or simply curious about Google's powerful apps, this book will give you the confidence to use them effortlessly. With this guide, you'll discover how to stay organized, collaborate smoothly, and boost productivity—at work, at school, or in everyday life.

Table of Contents

PART ONE

Getting Started with Google Workspace

Chapter One

Introduction to Google Workspace: An All-in-One Productivity Suite

G oogle Workspace is a comprehensive suite of tools designed to enhance productivity, communication, and collaboration for both personal use and business. This chapter will walk you through the core features and functions of Google Workspace, providing a foundational understanding of its value, how it compares to free alternatives, and the various subscription options available.

What Exactly Is Google Workspace?

Google Workspace (formerly known as G Suite) is a collection of productivity and collaboration tools developed by Google. It integrates various essential services such as Gmail, Google Drive, Google Docs, Google Meet, and many others, all within a single platform. These tools are designed to help users create, store, share, and collaborate on documents, emails, calendars, and more—all in real time.

Google Workspace is used by individuals, businesses, and organizations of all sizes, making work more efficient and helping teams communicate seamlessly.

Google Workspace vs. Free Google Apps: What's the Difference?

While Google offers a variety of free apps (like Gmail, Google Drive, and Google Docs), Google Workspace takes these tools to the next level by offering additional features tailored for professionals and businesses.

- **Additional Features**: With Google Workspace, you get access to advanced security features, increased cloud storage, business email addresses (e.g., yourname@yourcompany.com), and enhanced support.
- **Customization**: Google Workspace allows greater customization in terms of branding, such as using your company's logo on Gmail signatures or custom URLs for Google Meet and Drive.
- **Business Tools**: Google Workspace offers tools like Google Admin Console to manage users, roles, and security settings, something not available with free apps.
- **Collaboration**: With features like unlimited Google Meet sessions, Google Chat for instant messaging, and advanced document collaboration in real time, Google Workspace is designed for smooth team collaboration.

Key Benefits of Google Workspace for Personal Use & Business

For Individuals:

- **Access to Premium Features**: Use business-grade features, such as professional email, increased storage, and video conferencing.
- **Seamless Synchronization**: With a Google Workspace account, you can sync all your Google services (Gmail, Docs, Drive, etc.) across multiple devices, ensuring you're always connected.

For Businesses:

- **Collaboration & Productivity**: Google Workspace enables teams to work together effortlessly using Google Docs, Sheets, and Slides in real-time. The integration of Google Meet and Google Chat enhances communication.
- **Enhanced Security**: For business use, Google Workspace provides advanced security options like two-step verification, data loss prevention, and admin controls to keep your company's data safe.
- **Support & Reliability**: Google Workspace offers dedicated 24/7 support, ensuring that businesses have the assistance they need in case of any technical issues.

💡 *Tip: Google Workspace provides not only collaboration tools but also analytics and reporting features, which can be very useful for businesses to track productivity and performance.*

Understanding Google Workspace Pricing Plans

Google Workspace offers various pricing plans to cater to different types of users—from individuals to large businesses. Understanding these plans will help you determine which one fits your needs.

Plans Overview:

- **Business Starter**: This entry-level plan offers essential features such as business email, 30 GB of cloud storage per user, and video conferencing for up to 100 participants.
- **Business Standard**: Adds additional features such as 2 TB of cloud storage per user and enhanced video meeting capabilities with up to 150 participants.
- **Business Plus**: Includes advanced security and management controls, 5 TB of cloud storage, and video meetings with up to 250 participants.
- **Enterprise**: The top-tier plan with customized pricing, unlimited storage, advanced security tools, and enterprise-grade support.

💡 *Tip: If you're unsure which plan to choose, take advantage of Google's 14-day free trial to explore each option and decide which features are most beneficial for you.*

How to Sign Up for Google Workspace: A Step-by-Step Guide

Signing up for Google Workspace is quick and straightforward. Here's a simple guide to getting started:

1. **Visit the Google Workspace Website**: Go to https://workspace.google.com to start the sign-up process.

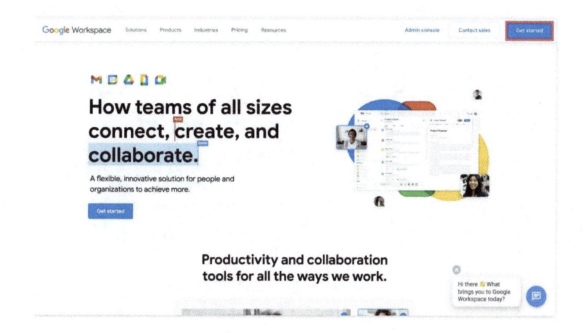

2. **Choose Your Plan**: Select the pricing plan that best fits your needs (Starter, Standard, Plus, or Enterprise).
3. **Create Your Account**: Enter your business name, the number of employees, and other relevant information.

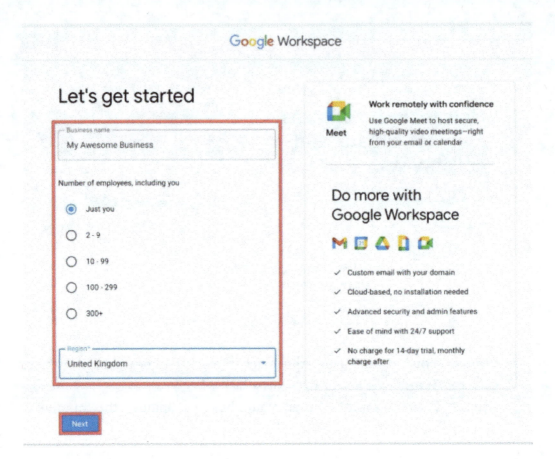

4. **Set Up Your Domain**: If you're using a custom domain (e.g., yourcompany.com), you'll need to verify ownership. If not, you can use a generic domain.

5. **Create User Accounts**: Set up accounts for all users who will be part of your Google Workspace environment.

6. **Configure Settings**: Customize your email, storage settings, and other preferences.

Once you complete these steps, you'll have full access to your Google Workspace dashboard, ready to begin using all the tools!

Navigating the Google Workspace Dashboard

The Google Workspace dashboard is your command center for managing your services and settings. Once logged in, you'll see quick links to key tools like Gmail, Google Drive, and Google Calendar.

- **Admin Console**: If you're the administrator, this is where you manage user accounts, settings, and security.
- **User Profile**: As a user, you'll have access to your profile settings and preferences for different apps.
- **App Access**: The dashboard allows you to easily access various Google Workspace apps and switch between them seamlessly.

💡 *Tip: Familiarize yourself with the dashboard layout to speed up navigation. The more you use it, the faster you'll get at managing your tasks and settings.*

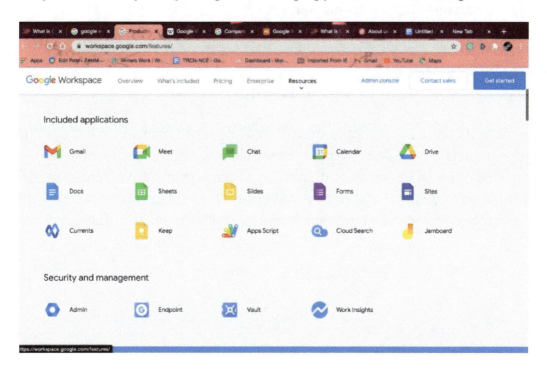

Switching Between Google Workspace Apps

Google Workspace apps work together in an integrated system, so switching between them is easy. Here's how to navigate:

1. **From Gmail to Drive**: When viewing an email with an attachment in Gmail, click the attachment to open it directly in Google Drive.
2. **From Google Meet to Calendar**: If you're in a meeting and want to schedule another one, simply switch to Google Calendar from within Google Meet.
3. **From Docs to Sheets**: You can quickly jump from Google Docs to Google Sheets by clicking the "Apps" icon at the top-right corner of the screen and selecting the app you want.

With seamless transitions between apps, you can stay productive without having to jump from one platform to another.

Conclusion

Google Workspace is a versatile suite of tools designed to enhance collaboration and productivity. By understanding the benefits, differences from free apps, pricing options, and how to set it up, you can harness the full potential of these tools for both personal and professional use. Throughout this book, we'll dive deeper into each individual tool, showing you how to use it to its fullest extent.

Chapter Two

Setting Up & Managing Your Google Account

S etting up your Google account correctly is the first step in unlocking the full potential of Google Workspace. This chapter will guide you through creating your account, configuring your profile, managing settings for security and privacy, and understanding Google's storage options.

Creating a Google Account

Before you can start using Google Workspace, you need a Google account. Here's how to get started:

1. **Visit the Google Sign-Up Page**: Go to https://accounts.google.com/signup.

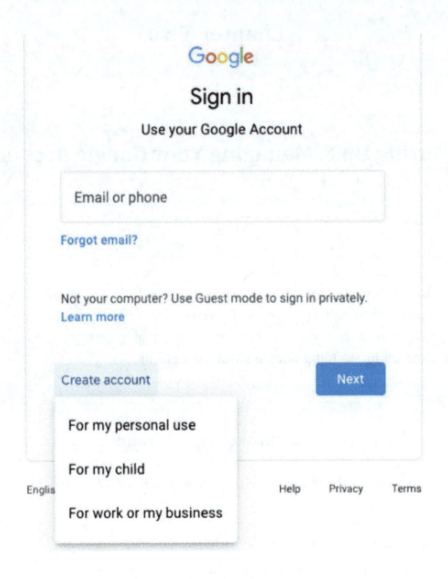

2. **Enter Your Information**: You'll need to provide details such as your name, desired email address, and a secure password.

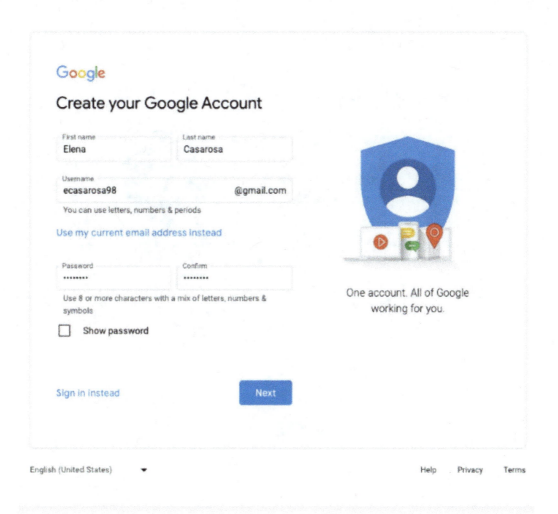

3. **Verify Your Account**: Google may ask for a phone number for account recovery and security. You'll also need to verify your phone number by entering a code sent via text message.

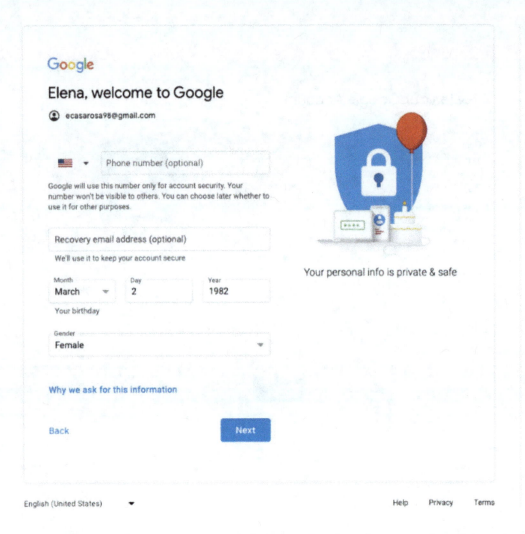

4. **Agree to the Terms & Conditions**: Read and accept Google's privacy policy and terms of service to finalize your registration.

Google

Privacy and Terms

To create a Google Account, you'll need to agree to the Terms of Service below.

In addition, when you create an account, we process your information as described in our Privacy Policy, including these key points:

Data we process when you use Google

- When you set up a Google Account, we store information you give us like your name, email address, and telephone number.
- When you use Google services to do things like write a message in Gmail or comment on a YouTube video, we store the information you create.
- When you search for a restaurant on Google Maps or watch a video on YouTube, for example, we process information about that activity – including information like the video you watched, device IDs, IP addresses, cookie data, and location.
- We also process the kinds of information described above when you use apps or sites that use Google services like ads, Analytics, and the YouTube video player.

You're in control of the data we collect & how it's used

Once your account is set up, you can access Google's entire suite of tools, including Gmail, Google Drive, and more.

Setting Up Your Profile Picture & Personal Information

Having a personalized profile helps you make the most of your Google account by allowing others to recognize you across services like Gmail, Google Meet, and Google Drive.

1. **Profile Picture**:
   - Go to your Google account settings and click on the **Profile Picture** section.

o   Upload a photo or select an image from your Google Photos.

💡 *Tip: Choose a clear, professional image if you're using your account for work purposes to maintain a polished appearance.*

2. **Personal Information**:
    o   Under **Personal Info**, update your name, contact info, and other details.
    o   You can also add a recovery email to help recover your account if you ever forget your password.

Managing Google Account Settings (Security, Privacy, & Notifications)

Once your account is set up, it's essential to adjust your settings for security, privacy, and notifications to keep your account safe and personalized.

Security Settings:

- **Two-Factor Authentication (2FA)**: Enabling 2FA adds an extra layer of protection by requiring a code in addition to your password to log in. This ensures that even if someone gets hold of your password, they won't be able to access your account without the second factor.
- **Password Management**: Consider using a password manager for strong and unique passwords across all your Google services.

Privacy Settings:

- **Reviewing Data Sharing Preferences**: Google allows you to manage what data is shared with third-party apps, as well as Google's use of your data. You can access these settings under **Privacy** in your Google Account.
- **Location & Activity Controls**: Control whether Google collects information like your search history or location data.

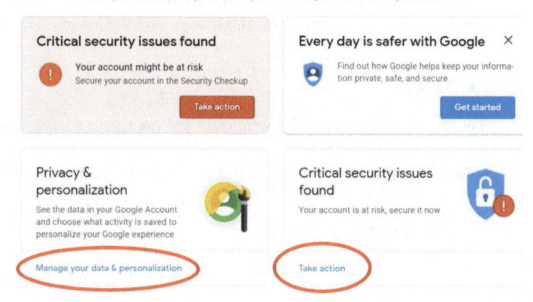

Notification Settings:

- **Email Notifications**: Adjust your notification preferences for Google services such as Gmail, Google Meet, and Google Calendar.
- **Push Notifications**: Set up push notifications for your mobile apps or through the Google website to stay informed.

💡 *Tip: Regularly review your security settings to ensure your account stays protected, especially after any significant changes to your information.*

Understanding Google Storage Plans & Upgrading Storage

Google offers a certain amount of free storage, but depending on your needs, you might want to upgrade your storage plan.

Free Storage:

- Google provides **15 GB** of free cloud storage across all services (Gmail, Google Drive, Google Photos, etc.). This is often enough for personal use but may not be sufficient for heavy business users.

Upgrading Storage:

- If you find that you're running low on space, you can purchase additional storage through Google One.
- **Google One** offers storage plans starting at **100 GB** and going up to **2 TB** or more, depending on your needs.
- You can upgrade your storage directly from your Google account or through the **Google One** app.

💡 *Tip: If you're storing a lot of photos or videos, consider using **Google Photos'** high-quality storage options to save space without compromising image quality.*

Conclusion

Setting up and managing your Google account is crucial for getting the most out of Google Workspace. By customizing your profile, securing your account, managing your privacy settings, and understanding your storage options, you'll be well on your way to using Google's services more efficiently and securely.

Chapter Three

Google Workspace Security & Privacy Settings

I n this chapter, we'll focus on securing your Google account and ensuring your privacy. With the increasing amount of sensitive information stored online, taking the right steps to protect your Google Workspace account is essential. We'll cover enabling two-factor authentication (2FA), managing recovery options, adjusting privacy settings, and reviewing connected apps to ensure your account remains secure and your data stays private.

Enabling Two-Factor Authentication (2FA)

Two-Factor Authentication (2FA) adds an extra layer of security to your Google Workspace account. With 2FA, even if someone learns your password, they cannot access your account without the second verification step, which is typically a code sent to your phone.

1. **Go to Security Settings**:
   - Open your Google account settings by visiting myaccount.google.com.
   - On the left side, click on **Security**.

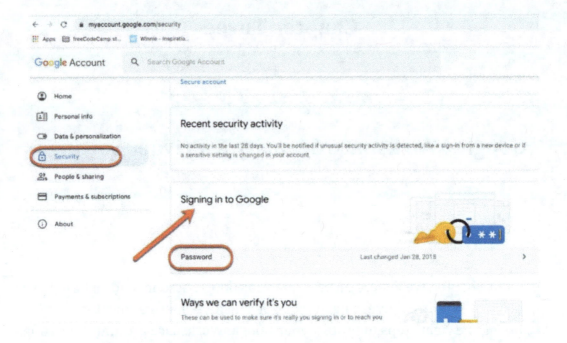

2. **Enable 2-Step Verification**:
   - Under the **Signing into Google** section, find and click on **2-Step Verification**.

Security Checkup

1 issue found

🟡 **2-Step Verification**
Add a backup second step   ⌄

✅ **Your devices**
2 signed-in devices   ⌄

✅ **Recent security events**
5 recent events   ⌄

---

o   Follow the on-screen prompts to set it up. You'll need to choose how
    you want to receive the verification code—either through your
    mobile phone number (text message or call) or by using a Google
    Authenticator app.

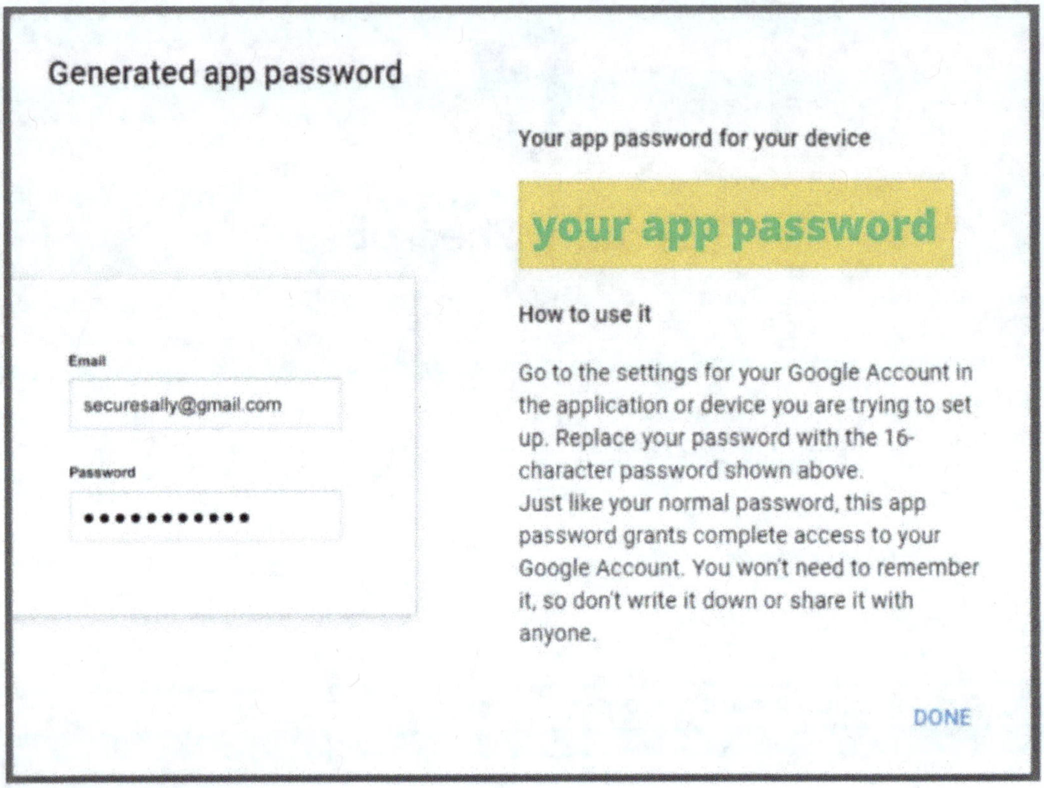

Generated app password

Your app password for your device

your app password

How to use it

Go to the settings for your Google Account in the application or device you are trying to set up. Replace your password with the 16-character password shown above.
Just like your normal password, this app password grants complete access to your Google Account. You won't need to remember it, so don't write it down or share it with anyone.

Email

securesally@gmail.com

Password

•••••••••••

DONE

3. **Backup Options**:
   o Google offers backup options like backup codes or a Google prompt to ensure you can still access your account if you lose your phone.
4. **Test & Confirm**: After setting up, it's a good idea to test that 2FA is working correctly by signing out and signing back in.

💡 *Tip: When using 2FA, always make sure your backup options are updated so you don't get locked out of your account.*

Managing Google Account Recovery Options

Account recovery is vital in case you forget your password or your account is compromised. By setting up recovery options, you can ensure that you can regain access to your Google Workspace account.

1. **Go to Account Recovery Settings**:
   - Visit your Google account settings at myaccount.google.com.
   - Under the **Security** section, click on **Recovery Options**.
2. **Add Recovery Email & Phone Number**:
   - You'll be asked to add a **recovery email** (an alternative email address that only you can access) and a **recovery phone number**. These will be used if you forget your password or need to confirm your identity.

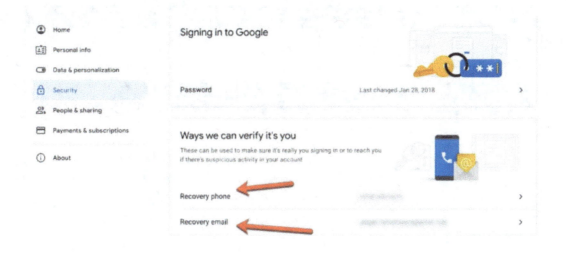

3. **Update Regularly**:
   - It's essential to keep your recovery email and phone number up to date. If these change, update them immediately to prevent being locked out of your account.

💡 *Tip: Use an email address that you check regularly and a phone number that is always with you to ensure you can recover your account without delay.*

Adjusting Privacy & Data Sharing Settings

Google provides several options for controlling what data is shared and how it's used. By adjusting your privacy settings, you can limit the amount of personal information Google collects and shares.

1. **Access Privacy Settings**:
   - From your Google account page, click on **Privacy** in the left sidebar.

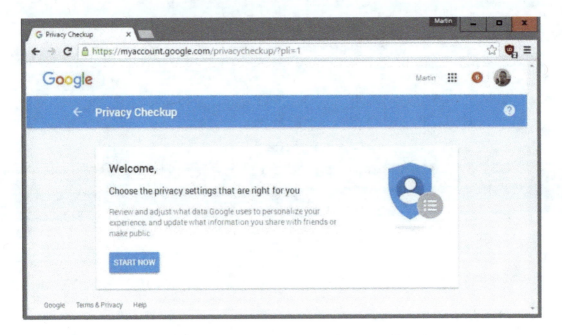

2. **Data & Personalization**:
   - You can control what data is collected by Google, such as search history, location data, and ad personalization. Adjust these settings based on your preferences:
     - **Activity Controls**: Turn off settings like Web & App Activity, Location History, and YouTube History if you don't want Google to track these.
     - **Ad Settings**: Decide whether Google can use your data to show you personalized ads.

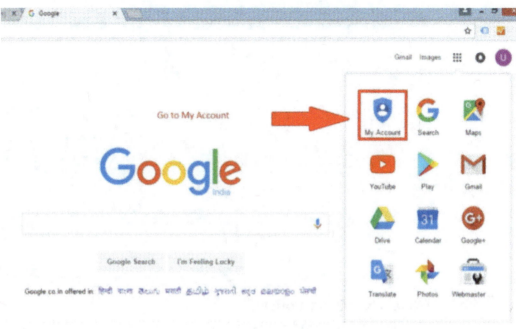

Welcome, ⬛⬛⬛⬛⬛⬛⬛⬛

Control, protect and secure your account, all in one place

u quick access to settings and tools that let you safeguard your data, protect your privacy and decide how your information can m
work better for you.

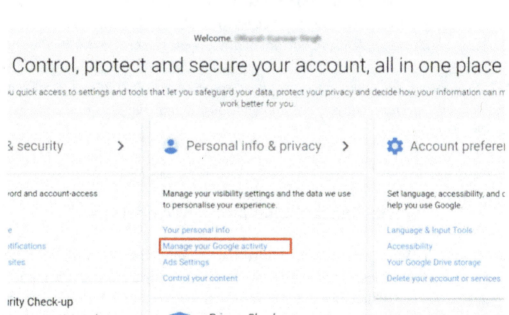

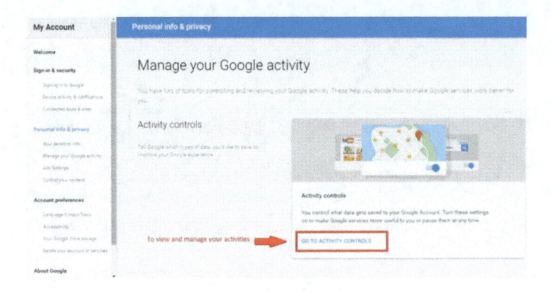

3. **Review Google's Privacy Policy**:
   o It's always a good idea to review Google's privacy policy periodically. You can access this policy through the **Privacy & Terms** link at the bottom of any Google page.

💡 *Tip: Limiting data sharing may affect some services' functionality, such as personalized search results or recommendations. Weigh the pros and cons before disabling features.*

Reviewing & Managing Connected Apps

Your Google account can connect to third-party applications that integrate with Google Workspace. These apps might have access to your data, and it's important to regularly review which ones have permission to interact with your account.

1. **Access Connected Apps**:
   o Go to the **Security** section of your Google account settings.
   o Scroll down to find the **Third-party apps with account access** section.
2. **Review Permissions**:

- Click on **Manage Third-party Access**. Here you'll see a list of apps that have access to your account.
- For each app, you can see what kind of permissions it has (such as accessing your Google Drive files or Gmail).
3. **Revoke Unnecessary Access**:
   - If you no longer use an app or don't trust it, click on it and select **Remove Access** to revoke its permissions.
4. **Stay Vigilant**:
   - Regularly check for any new apps that may have gained access to your Google account, and revoke access to apps you no longer use.

💡 *Tip: Always be cautious when granting permissions to third-party apps. Ensure they are reputable before granting access to your Google account.*

Conclusion

By taking the time to properly secure your Google Workspace account, you protect not only your personal information but also any business data stored across Google tools. Implementing two-factor authentication, managing recovery options, adjusting privacy settings, and keeping track of connected apps will greatly enhance the security of your account. Always stay proactive in reviewing these settings, as doing so is key to maintaining a safe and secure online experience.

PART TWO

Communication & Collaboration Tools

Chapter Four

Mastering Gmail – Your Go-To Email Platform

I n this chapter, we'll explore how to harness the full potential of Gmail, Google's powerful email tool. Gmail is more than just an inbox—it offers a wide range of features to help you manage your emails efficiently, stay organized, and improve your productivity. Let's dive into the essential tips and techniques for using Gmail to its fullest.

Overview of the Gmail Interface

When you open Gmail, you'll see the main email screen that consists of several key sections:

1. **Inbox**: The default section where new messages arrive.
2. **Sidebar**: On the left, you'll find labels like Inbox, Sent, Drafts, Spam, and more.
3. **Search Bar**: At the top, use this to find specific emails by keywords, senders, or dates.
4. **Settings Gear**: On the right side, click the gear icon to access settings.

💡 *Tip: Use the search bar to quickly locate important emails—Google's search algorithms are powerful, and you can search by almost any criteria (sender, date, attachments, etc.).*

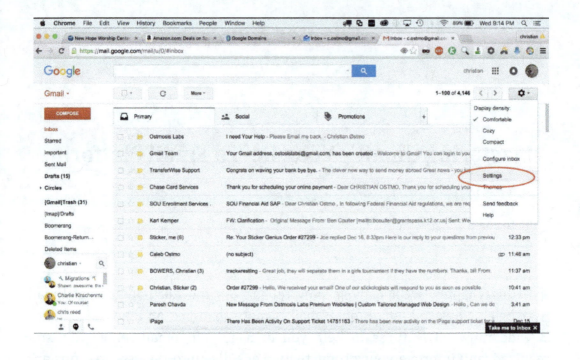

Composing & Formatting Emails with Precision

Gmail provides simple but effective tools to compose and format your emails:

1. **Compose a New Email**:
   ○ Click on the **Compose** button in the top left to start writing an email.

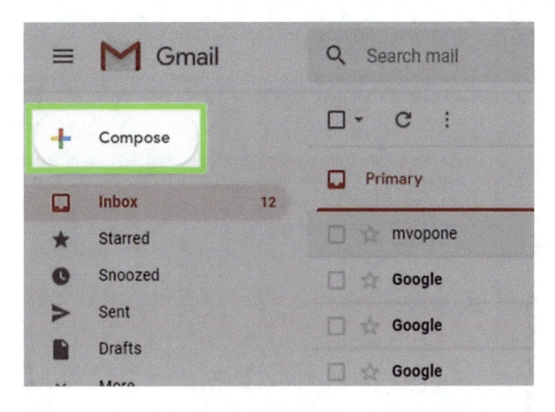

- o Enter the recipient's email address in the "To" field. You can also add people in the **CC** or **BCC** fields for mass emails.
2. **Formatting Tools**:
    - o Use the **Text formatting** toolbar to adjust font style, size, color, and alignment.
    - o Add bullet points, numbered lists, and hyperlinks for better structure and clarity.
    - o You can also attach files by clicking on the **paperclip icon** at the bottom.

💡 *Tip: Use **rich formatting** options for a professional look, but avoid over-cluttering your email. Keep it simple and to the point.*

Organizing Emails with Labels, Filters, & Stars

Keeping your inbox tidy is crucial, and Gmail makes it easy to organize your emails through several powerful features:

1. **Labels**:
   - Labels are like folders, but you can apply multiple labels to a single email.
   - To create a label, click on an email, then click the **Labels** icon at the top to create and assign new labels.

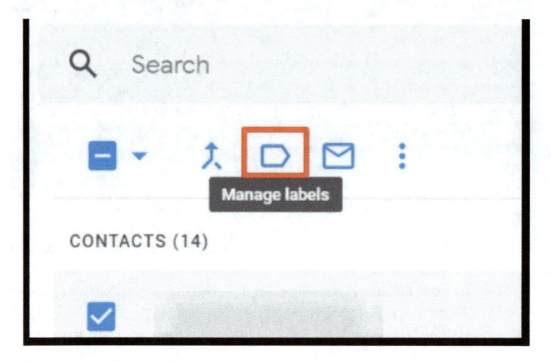

2. **Filters**:
   - Filters help you automatically organize incoming emails. For example, you can create a filter that automatically labels all emails from your boss as "Work" or moves newsletters to a separate folder.
   - To create a filter, click on the **Search Bar** and then click the downward-facing arrow to access advanced search. Choose your filter criteria and click **Create filter**.

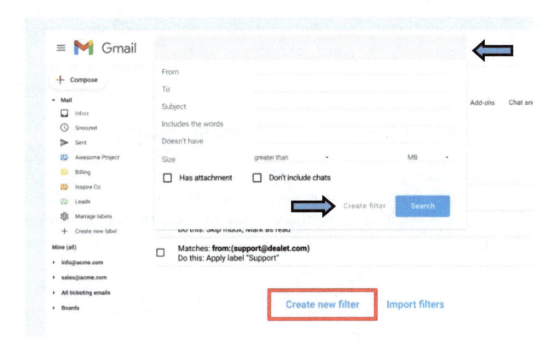

3. **Stars**:

- o Stars are a great way to mark important emails. You can click the **Star** icon next to an email to mark it, making it easier to find later.

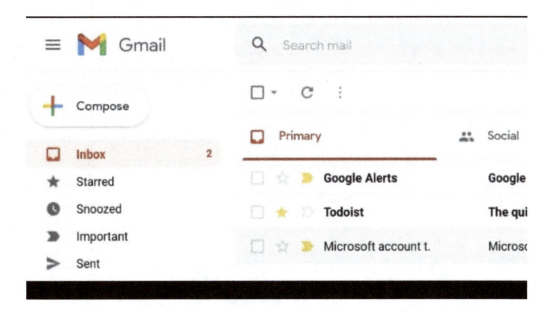

💡 *Tip: Use **multiple stars** (you can enable different colors and types of stars in settings) to categorize emails based on urgency or priority.*

Setting Up Auto-Replies & Email Signatures

1. **Auto-Replies**:
    - Set up automatic replies when you're away or out of the office. To enable this, go to **Settings > Vacation responder** and enable the feature.

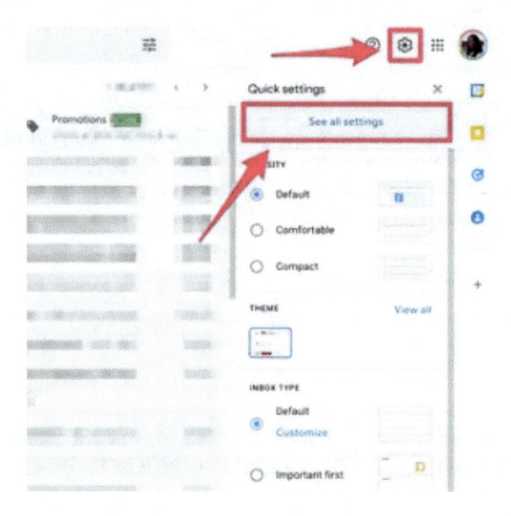

o You can specify the start and end dates, and create a message that will be sent automatically to people who email you during that period.

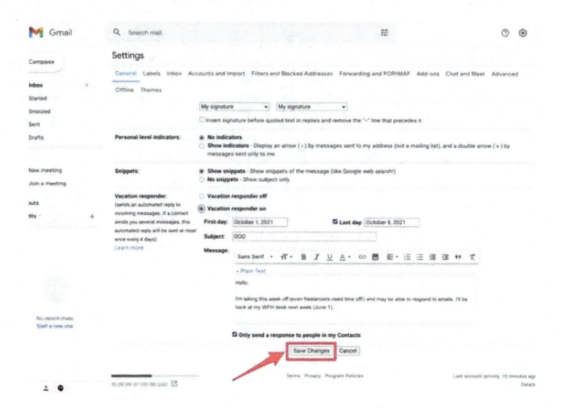

2. **Email Signatures**:
   o An email signature provides contact details or a professional closing for your emails. To set it up, go to **Settings > Signature** and enter the text you want to appear at the end of every email you send.

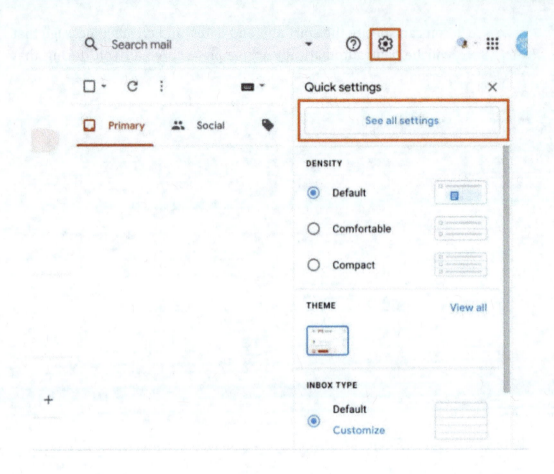

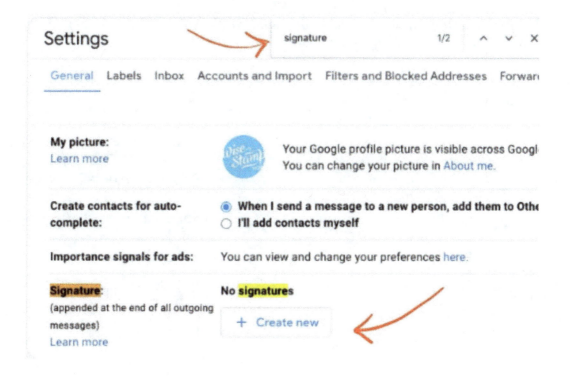

💡 *Tip: Personalize your auto-replies and signatures to reflect your professional tone and make your responses feel more personal.*

Using Gmail Shortcuts for Faster Navigation

Gmail offers several shortcuts to help you navigate quickly:

1. **Enable Keyboard Shortcuts**:
   - Go to **Settings > See all settings > General > Keyboard shortcuts** and select **Enable**.
2. **Common Shortcuts**:
   - Press **C** to compose a new email.
   - Press **E** to archive an email.
   - Press **/ (forward slash)** to jump to the search bar.

Tip: Mastering Gmail shortcuts can significantly improve your workflow and reduce time spent navigating the interface.

Shortcut	Function
C	Compose new email
R	Reply to an email
F	Forward an email
Ctrl + Enter	Send email
E	Archive email
Shift + U	Mark as unread

Scheduling Emails for Later Delivery

Gmail allows you to compose an email and schedule it for later delivery, which can be useful for managing time-sensitive messages:

1. **Compose your email** and click the **Send** button.
2. **Click the small arrow** next to the send button and select **Schedule send**.

example@mail.com

How to Schedule an Email in Gmail on Desktop

Hi John,
Hope this meets you well. This is a step-by-step guide on how to schedule an email in Gmail on your desktop computer.

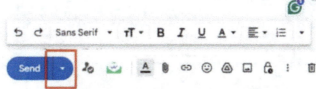

How to Schedule an Email in Gmail on Desktop

example@mail.com

How to Schedule an Email in Gmail on Desktop

Hi John,
Hope this meets you well. This is a step-by-step guide on how to schedule an email in Gmail on your desktop computer.

3. Choose the date and time you'd like the email to be sent.

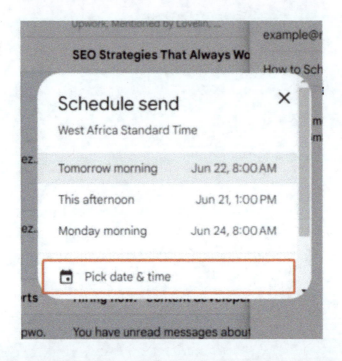

Tip: Use this feature to send emails at optimal times, such as early in the morning or during business hours, even if you're working outside of those times.

Managing Spam & Unwanted Emails

Gmail helps protect you from spam, but it's important to know how to manage and clean up your inbox:

1. **Mark Emails as Spam**:
   - If an email looks suspicious, click the **three vertical dots** in the upper-right corner of the email and select **Report spam**.
2. **Block Unwanted Senders**:
   - If you receive repeated unwanted emails, you can block the sender by clicking the **three dots** on their email and selecting **Block**.
3. **Unsubscribe**:
   - Gmail provides an **Unsubscribe** button for certain promotional emails, which helps you avoid unwanted newsletters and offers.

Tip: Regularly clean your spam folder and unsubscribe from irrelevant mailing lists to keep your inbox clutter-free.

Conclusion

Mastering Gmail is about more than just sending and receiving emails. It's about streamlining your email management process, staying organized, and boosting your productivity with the various features Gmail provides. By leveraging Gmail's full suite of tools, you'll find your inbox less cluttered and your workflow much more efficient.

Chapter Five

Google Chat – Streamlining Instant Messaging & Team Collaboration

---

I n this chapter, we'll explore **Google Chat**, a powerful tool designed to facilitate quick communication and seamless collaboration within teams. Whether you're managing a project, discussing tasks, or sharing updates, Google Chat is the perfect platform to keep your conversations organized and efficient. Let's dive into how to leverage its features to enhance teamwork.

Navigating the Google Chat Interface

The Google Chat interface is simple and user-friendly, designed for seamless communication. Here's a breakdown of the main components:

- **Left Sidebar**: This section shows your direct messages (DMs), spaces (group chats), and other areas like the **Home** and **Rooms** (if applicable).
- **Chat Window**: The central area displays your current conversations, where you can send and receive messages.
- **Search Bar**: Located at the top, use this to find conversations, spaces, or messages by keywords.

💡 *Tip: Use the search bar for quick navigation between chats and to find messages that are hard to locate.*

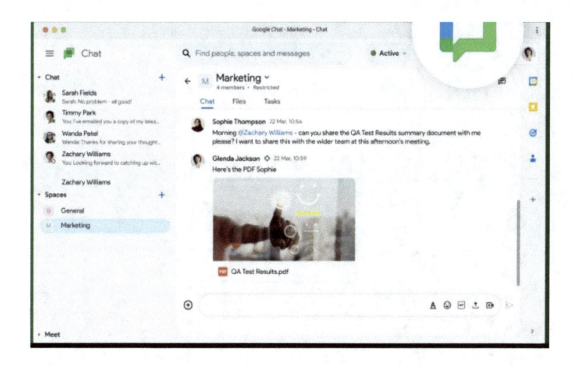

Starting & Managing Conversations

1. **Start a New Conversation**:
    o   To begin a one-on-one conversation, click on the **"+" icon** (New Chat) on the left sidebar. Enter the person's name or email, and hit enter to start chatting.

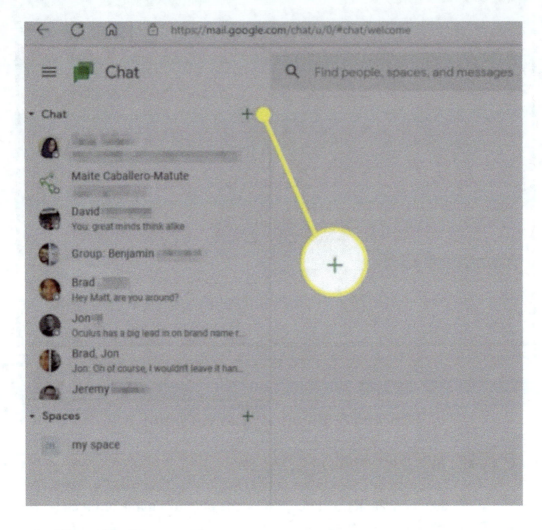

2. **Managing Conversations**:

   ○ You can **pin** important conversations for easy access. Simply hover over the conversation, click the **three dots**, and choose **Pin**.

   ○ Use **archiving** to keep your sidebar uncluttered. Archiving removes a conversation from the main view without deleting it.

💡 *Tip: Pinning essential conversations, like ongoing projects or key team discussions, keeps them readily accessible.*

Collaborating with Group Chats & Spaces

1. **Group Chats**:
   o Group chats are great for team discussions. You can add multiple participants by selecting the **"+" icon** and entering their emails.
   o Name the group chat to make it easier to identify.
2. **Spaces**:
   o Spaces allow teams to collaborate more effectively. They act as organized group chats where you can discuss topics, share files, and track progress.
   o To create a Space, click on the **+** sign and select **Create Space**. Then, name your space and add participants.

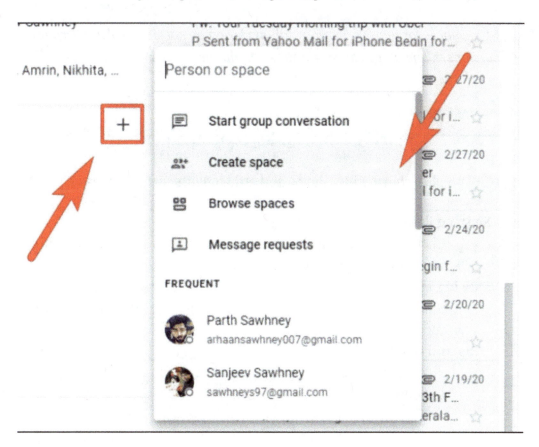

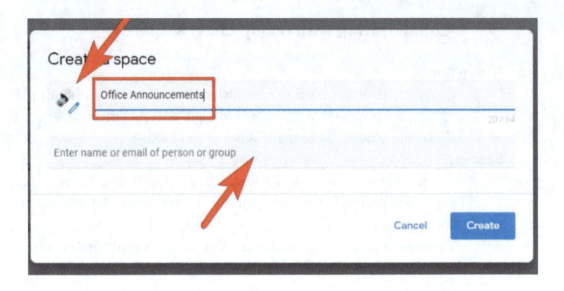

💡 *Tip: Use spaces for long-term team collaboration on specific projects. Organizing all discussions in one place can streamline communication.*

Sharing Files, Links, & Attachments

Google Chat makes sharing files, links, and attachments incredibly easy:

1. **Sharing Files**:
   - Click the **paperclip icon** in the message window to attach a file from your computer or Google Drive.
2. **Sharing Links**:
   - Simply paste the URL into the message, and it will automatically turn into a clickable link.
3. **Drag and Drop**:
   - For quick access, you can **drag and drop** files directly into the chat window.

💡 *Tip: Use Google Drive integration to share larger files and collaborate in real time on documents, spreadsheets, and presentations.*

Integrating Google Chat with Gmail

Google Chat and Gmail are deeply integrated, allowing for smooth transitions between emails and instant messaging:

1. **Accessing Google Chat from Gmail**:
   o In Gmail, you'll see a Google Chat section on the left side. You can use this to start chats or join ongoing conversations without leaving Gmail.
2. **Email Notifications for Google Chat**:
   o You can set up email notifications for when someone messages you in Google Chat, ensuring you never miss an important update.

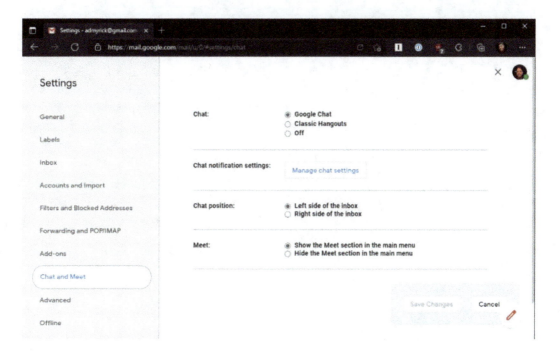

3. **Replying to Emails in Google Chat**:
   o If you receive an email that sparks a quick conversation, you can reply directly from within Google Chat without opening Gmail.

💡 *Tip: Use the Gmail and Google Chat integration to quickly move between email conversations and real-time chat without losing context.*

Conclusion

Google Chat is a powerful messaging tool that helps teams stay connected and organized. By mastering its features—like managing conversations, collaborating in spaces, sharing files, and integrating with Gmail—you can streamline communication and enhance your team's productivity. Whether for quick discussions or long-term project management, Google Chat simplifies collaboration and boosts efficiency.

Chapter Six

Google Meet – Hosting & Managing Video Calls with Ease

I n this chapter, we will explore **Google Meet**, Google's premier video conferencing platform, perfect for hosting virtual meetings, collaborating with teams, and connecting with others. Whether you're hosting a one-on-one video call or a large team presentation, Google Meet offers a seamless experience with user-friendly features. Let's dive into the steps for setting up and managing successful video meetings.

Setting Up a Google Meet Video Call

Getting started with a Google Meet video call is simple and straightforward. Here's a step-by-step guide:

1. **Access Google Meet**:
   o Open Google Meet by navigating to meet.google.com or accessing it through the Google apps menu in Gmail or Google Calendar.
2. **Start a New Meeting**:
   o Click on **"New Meeting"** and choose one of the following options:
      ▪ **Create a Meeting for Later**: This generates a meeting link that you can share with participants to join later.

- **Start an Instant Meeting**: Starts a meeting immediately, allowing you to invite participants on the fly.
- **Schedule in Google Calendar**: Set up a meeting in advance with all the details, including time, participants, and agenda.

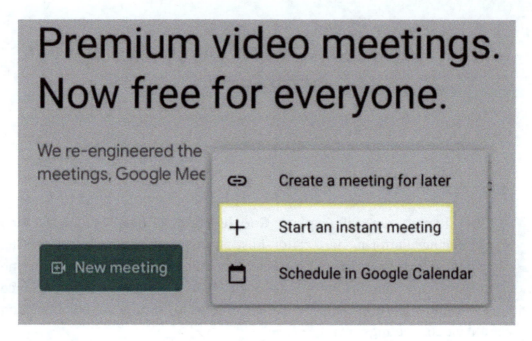

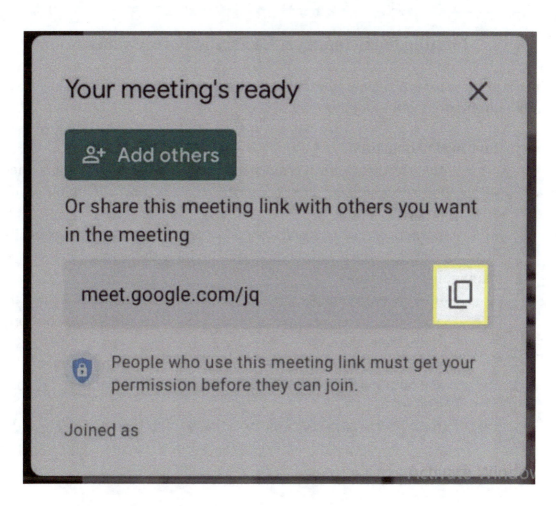

3. **Join an Existing Meeting**:
    - If you've been invited to a meeting, click on the **meeting link** or enter the **meeting code** on the Google Meet homepage to join the session.

💡 *Tip: Scheduling meetings in advance through Google Calendar allows for seamless integration, with meeting links and participant invitations automatically generated.*

Inviting Participants & Managing Permissions

Inviting others to your Google Meet call and managing their permissions ensures a smooth and productive meeting experience:

1. **Inviting Participants**:
   o After starting the meeting, click on **"Add Others"** and share the generated meeting link via email, chat, or any communication platform.
   o Alternatively, you can directly add participants using their email addresses, which will send them an invite with the link.
2. **Managing Permissions**:
   o **Mute Participants**: As the host, you can mute other participants if background noise becomes a distraction. Click the **"Mute"** button next to their name.
   o **Control Camera Access**: You can choose to **turn off** someone's camera if needed, especially if there's a bandwidth issue or distractions.
   o **Allow Participants to Join**: You can enable the **"Quick Access"** feature for automatic entry, or choose to manually admit people from the waiting room.

💡 *Tip: Before the meeting, remind participants to check their audio and video settings to avoid technical issues during the call.*

Enhancing Your Video Call with Background Effects & Filters

Google Meet offers several ways to enhance your video presence with **background effects** and **filters**:

1. **Using Background Effects**:
   o Click on the **three vertical dots** (More options) in the bottom right corner, then select **Change Background**.

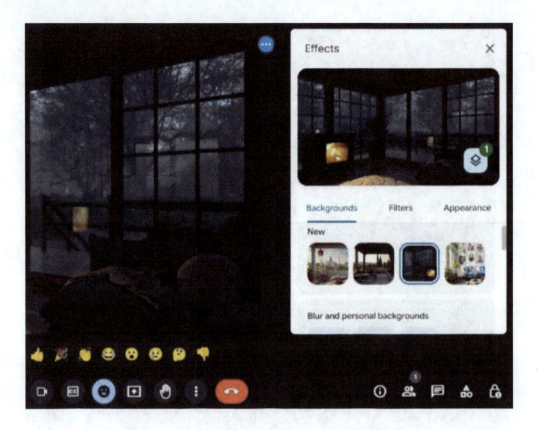

- o You can blur your background, choose from available virtual backgrounds, or even upload your own custom background.
2. **Using Filters**:
   - o In addition to background effects, Google Meet lets you apply **filters** to your video stream, such as adjusting lighting, applying color filters, and other fun effects to enhance your look.
   - o These features can help you maintain a professional appearance in less-than-ideal environments or add a personal touch to your calls.

💡 *Tip: Use background effects sparingly to avoid distractions. A subtle background blur is often sufficient for professional calls.*

Sharing Your Screen & Presenting Slides

Google Meet makes it easy to share your screen and present content in real-time during your meeting:

1. **Sharing Your Screen**:
   o Click the **Present Now** button at the bottom of the screen and choose whether you want to share your entire screen, a specific window, or a Chrome tab.
   o If you choose **Present Chrome Tab**, any open tab will be shared, making it ideal for presentations involving websites or videos.

2. **Presenting Slides**:
   o Open your Google Slides, click **Slideshow** drop-down button. Click on **Presenter view**.

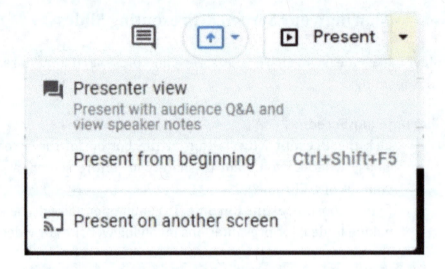

- o Then go back to Google Meet, share your entire screen or a specific window with the slides displayed.

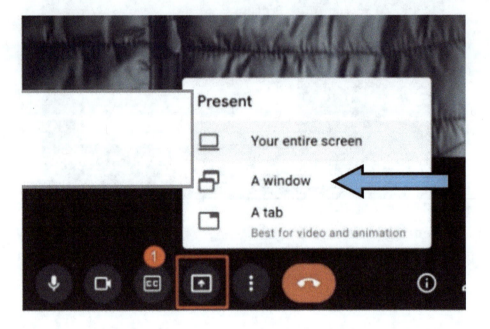

From the options, choose the Google Slides window and select **Share.**

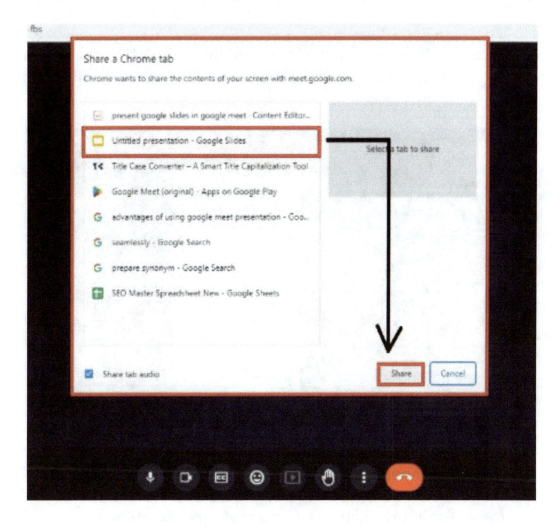

- o You can control the presentation directly from Google Meet, allowing for smooth transitions and seamless presentations.

💡 *Tip: For a smoother experience, close unnecessary tabs and apps before sharing your screen to avoid interruptions and reduce lag.*

Recording & Saving Meetings

Google Meet allows you to record your meetings, making it easier to revisit discussions or share them with absentees:

1. **Starting a Recording**:
   - As the meeting host, click on the **three vertical dots** and select **Record Meeting**. All participants will be notified when the recording starts.

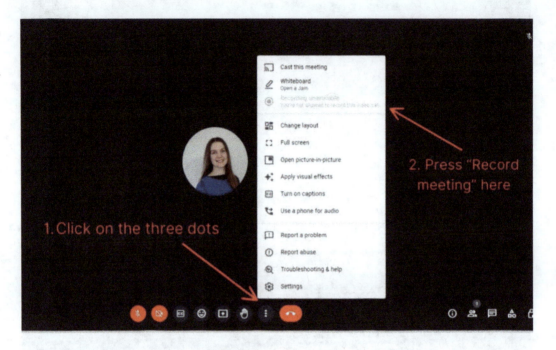

2. **Saving & Sharing Recordings**:
   - The recorded meeting will automatically be saved to the host's Google Drive under a folder named **"Meet Recordings"**.
   - You can share the recording by right-clicking on the file in Google Drive and selecting **Get link**, or directly sending the file to participants.
3. **Accessing Recordings**:
   - Once the recording is processed, it will appear in the host's Google Drive. You'll receive an email notification with a link to access the recording.

💡 *Tip: Be sure to get consent from meeting participants before recording to ensure transparency and respect for privacy.*

Conclusion

Google Meet offers a robust platform for hosting video meetings and collaborating in real time. From setting up meetings and inviting participants to sharing screens and recording calls, mastering Google Meet's features can elevate your virtual collaboration experience. Whether you're holding a team meeting, conducting a one-on-one, or presenting a webinar, these tools make it easy to manage every aspect of your video conference efficiently.

PART THREE

Productivity & File Management

Chapter Seven

Google Drive – Organizing, Storing, & Sharing Files Effortlessly

---

In this chapter, we will explore **Google Drive**, your go-to cloud storage solution for storing, organizing, and sharing files. Whether you're managing personal documents or collaborating with teams, Google Drive provides a user-friendly environment to keep all your files accessible and secure. Let's break down how to make the most of Google Drive's features for seamless file management.

Uploading & Downloading Files in Google Drive

Getting your files into and out of Google Drive is quick and simple:

1. **Uploading Files**:
   - To upload files, click on the **"New"** button in the top-left corner of Google Drive and select **"File upload"** or **"Folder upload"**.

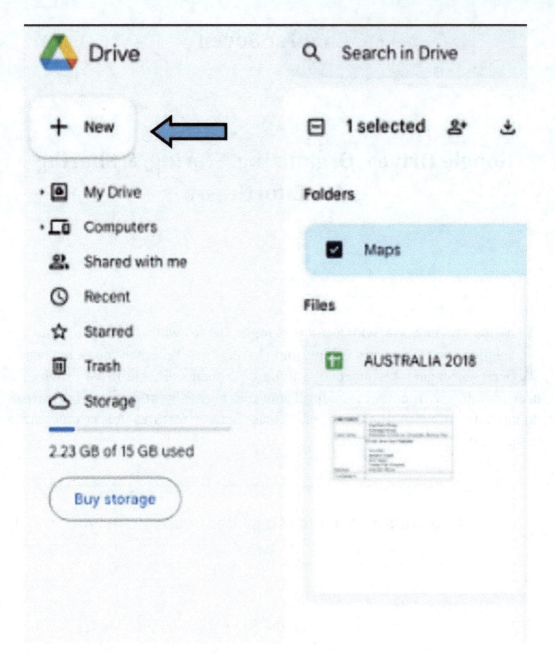

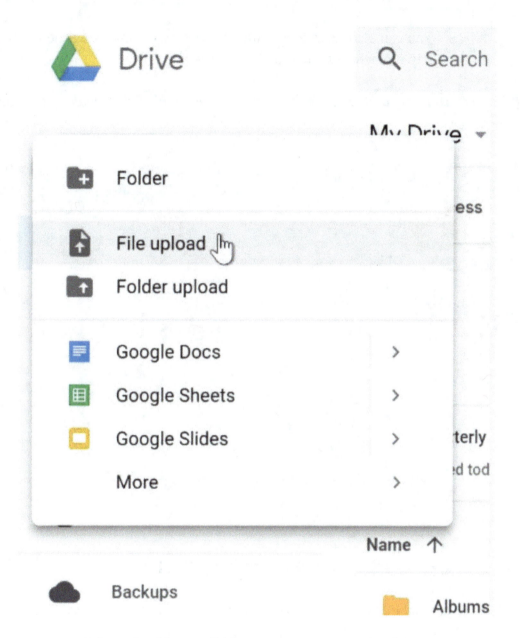

- o Select the files or folders you want to upload from your device. Google Drive supports multiple file types, including documents, images, videos, and more.
2. **Downloading Files**:
   - o To download a file, right-click on the file you wish to download and select **"Download"**. The file will be saved to your device's default download folder.

      o   You can also download entire folders by compressing them into a **.zip** file before saving to your device.

💡 *Tip: You can drag and drop files directly into the Google Drive window to upload them faster.*

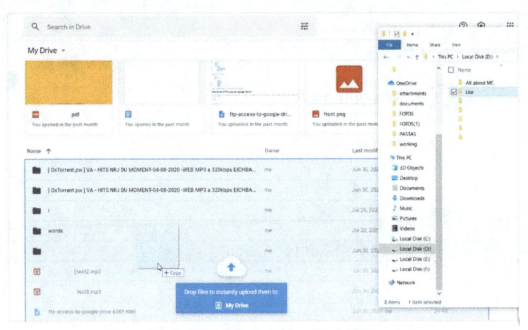

Drag and Drop Files from PC to Google Drive

Creating & Organizing Folders

A clean, organized Drive makes it easier to find and manage your files:

1. **Creating Folders**:
        o   Click on the **"New"** button and select **"Folder"**. Give the folder a descriptive name, and it will appear in your Google Drive for easy access.

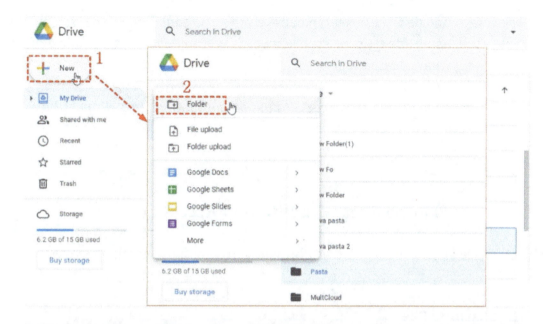

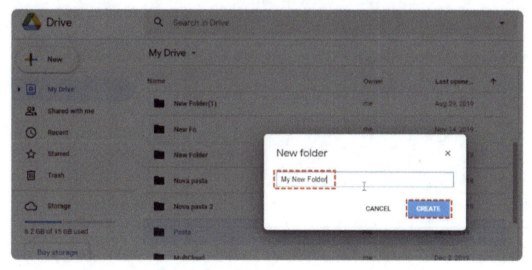

2. **Organizing Files & Folders**:
   - Drag and drop files into folders to keep them organized. You can create a hierarchy of folders to separate your work by project, department, or category.
   - Use **color coding** or custom names for folders to make them easy to spot.
3. **Searching for Files**:

o   Google Drive's search bar is a powerful tool. You can search by file name, file type, or even keywords within documents to quickly find what you need.

💡 *Tip: Organize folders with consistent naming conventions (e.g., Project Name – Date) to enhance file retrieval.*

Sharing Files with Different Access Levels

Google Drive allows you to control who sees your files and how they interact with them:

1. **Sharing a File**:
   o   Right-click on the file you wish to share and select **"Share"**.

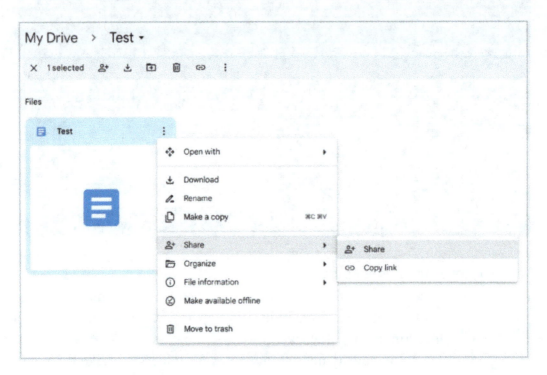

o   You can share via email by entering email addresses or get a shareable link that can be distributed.

2. **Setting Permissions**:
   - You can assign three access levels to the people you share your file with:
     - **Viewer**: Can view the file but not edit or comment.
     - **Commenter**: Can view and comment on the file but cannot make edits.
     - **Editor**: Can make changes to the file, including edits and additions.

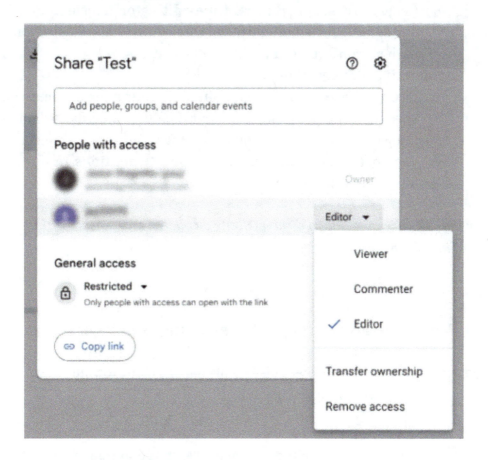

3. **Advanced Sharing Settings**:
   - Click on the **gear icon** in the share settings to manage whether editors can change permissions or share the file further.

💡 *Tip: For sensitive files, consider setting the file to **"View Only"** and disabling the option to download or print the file.*

Collaborating on Shared Files

Collaboration is easy in Google Drive, allowing multiple users to work on the same file simultaneously:

1. **Real-Time Collaboration**:
   - Google Drive supports **real-time editing** on Google Docs, Sheets, and Slides. When multiple people are editing a file at once, you'll see each person's cursor in a different color.
2. **Commenting & Suggesting**:
   - In **Google Docs** and **Google Sheets**, you can leave comments on specific sections of the document. Use the **"Suggesting"** mode in Google Docs to propose edits that others can accept or decline.
   - Tag collaborators in comments using **@mentions** to draw their attention to specific points.

💡 *Tip: Use "@" in comments to directly notify a collaborator, ensuring that they're aware of important changes or feedback.*

Managing File Versions & Restoring Older Versions

Google Drive automatically keeps a history of changes made to your files, allowing you to revert to earlier versions if needed:

1. **Viewing Version History**:
   - Right-click on the file and select **"Manage versions"** to view a list of previous versions.
   - You can view and download earlier versions of a file, making it easy to track changes over time.
2. **Restoring Older Versions**:

o If you need to revert to a previous version, click on the **three dots** next to the version you want to restore and select **"Restore this version"**.

💡 *Tip: Version history is especially useful for collaborative documents where multiple users make frequent edits.*

Google Drive Keyboard Shortcuts

Maximize your efficiency by using keyboard shortcuts for navigating Google Drive:

- **Quickly open the search bar**: Press /
- **Create a new file or folder**: Press **Shift + T** (for Docs) or **Shift + F** (for folders)
- **Navigate between files**: Use **arrow keys** to move up or down.
- **Preview a file**: Press **Enter** to preview a selected file.
- **Open the Google Drive menu**: Press **G** then **M**.

💡 *Tip: Learning these shortcuts can save you time and make your workflow smoother, especially when managing large numbers of files.*

Action	Shortcut (Windows & Mac)
Create a new folder	Shift + F
Upload a file	U
Open file preview	P
Rename a file	N
Select multiple files	Shift + Click
Search Google Drive	/
Open sharing settings	.
Delete a file	Delete

💡 *Tip: Press "Shift + ?" in Google Drive to view all shortcuts.*

Conclusion

Google Drive offers a robust, cloud-based platform for managing all your files—whether you're working solo or collaborating with a team. By mastering the essentials of uploading, organizing, sharing, and collaborating, you can stay on top of your file management tasks with ease. With advanced features like version history and real-time collaboration, Google Drive makes it simple to maintain control over your documents while ensuring productivity.

Chapter Eight

Google Docs – Crafting & Editing Documents with Ease

Google Docs provides a versatile platform for creating, editing, and collaborating on documents in real-time. Whether you're drafting a report, writing a story, or preparing a presentation, Google Docs offers a range of powerful tools and features to streamline the process. In this chapter, we'll explore the various ways you can create and format documents, as well as collaborate efficiently with others.

Navigating Google Docs Interface

Before you dive into creating your document, it's essential to familiarize yourself with the Google Docs interface:

1. **Toolbar**:
   - Located at the top of your document, the **toolbar** provides quick access to basic editing tools like **bold**, **italic**, **underline**, and **font size**.
2. **Menu Bar**:
   - The **menu bar** contains more advanced options such as **File**, **Edit**, **View**, and **Tools**. This is where you can find settings like **Page Setup** and **Word Count**.

3. **Document Area**:
   - The **main document area** is where you'll type your content. It offers a clean, distraction-free workspace to focus on your writing.
4. **Sidebar**:
   - On the right, the **sidebar** houses features like **Google Docs' outline** and **add-ons**.

💡 *Tip: To maximize screen space, you can hide the menu bar by selecting **View > Compact Controls**.*

Formatting Text, Paragraphs, & Styles

Creating well-structured documents requires more than just typing text. Formatting helps organize your ideas and makes your document easier to read:

1. **Text Formatting**:
   - You can format your text by using the **Formatting toolbar** for bold, italics, underline, text color, and highlighting.
   - Use **font styles** to give your document a consistent look.

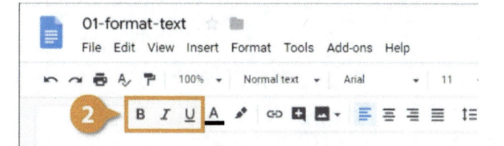

Ms. Robin Banks
Director of Community Engagement
ABC Enterprise
3562 E. Shady Oaks Ave.

Dear Mrs. Banks,

My name is Kayla and I've been selected by the school
to coordinate this year's cook-off to raise money for cla
community event will take place this summer at Highla
local chefs and musicians.

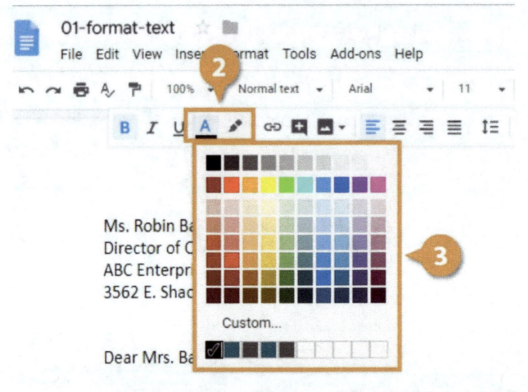

My name is Kayla and I've been selected by the school di
to coordinate this year's cook-off to raise money for class
community event will take place this summer at Highland
local chefs and musicians.

2. **Paragraph Formatting**:
   - Adjust paragraph alignment (left, center, right) and line spacing.
   - To create lists, use the **bulleted** or **numbered list** options.
3. **Using Styles**:
   - Google Docs provides **Heading styles** (Heading 1, Heading 2, etc.) for easy document structure. These headings not only format your document but also help create an outline.

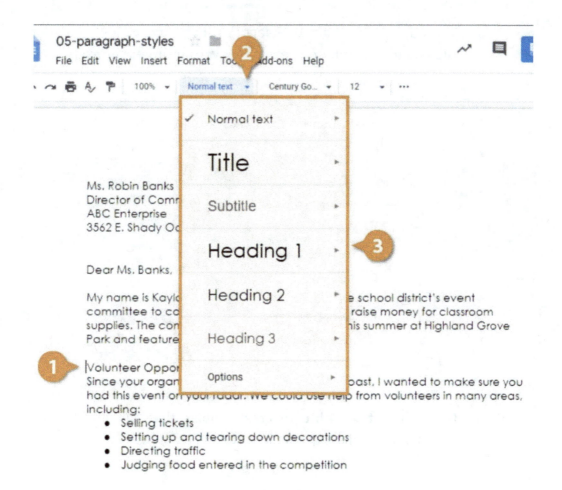

Tip: Using Heading styles enhances document accessibility and allows you to create a clickable outline in the sidebar for easy navigation.

Inserting Images, Tables, Links & Footnotes

Enhance your document with various media and elements to support your content:

1. **Inserting Images**:

- To add an image, go to **Insert > Image** and choose the source (upload from computer, search the web, or drag-and-drop).

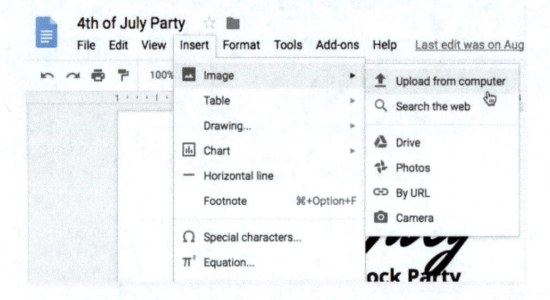

2. **Creating Tables**:
   - Go to **Insert > Table** to create tables that can help organize information or display data in rows and columns.

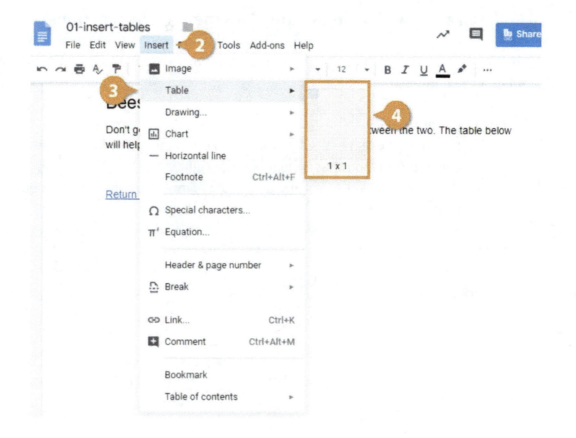

3. **Adding Links**:
   - ○ Highlight the text you want to link and click on the **Insert link** icon in the toolbar. Enter the URL or choose a bookmark from your document.
4. **Footnotes**:
   - ○ To insert footnotes, place your cursor where you want the footnote and select **Insert > Footnote**. This feature is great for citations and additional references.

💡 *Tip: To keep your document uncluttered, use images and tables sparingly and make sure they are relevant to the content.*

Collaborating with Others Using Comments & Suggestions

Google Docs is built for collaboration. You can easily work with others on the same document in real time:

1. **Adding Comments**:
   - Highlight the text or area you want to comment on and click the **Add comment** button that appears on the right side.
   - You can tag collaborators using the **@mention** to direct their attention.

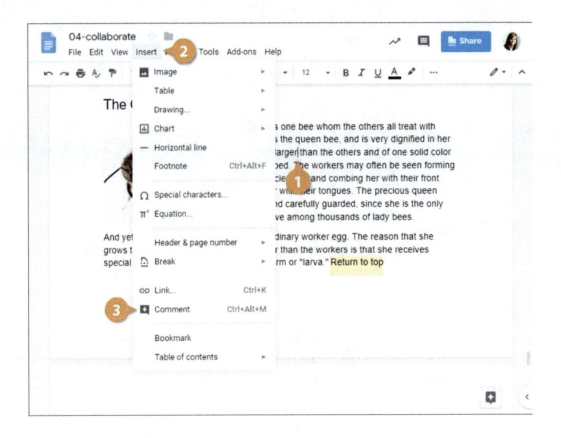

2. **Suggesting Edits**:
   - Switch to **Suggesting mode** by clicking on the pencil icon in the top-right corner. In this mode, any changes you make will appear as suggestions, which the document owner can approve or reject.

3. **Resolving Comments**:
   - o Once a comment or suggestion has been addressed, click the **Resolve** button to mark it as complete.

💡 *Tip: Use "@" to mention specific people in comments. This ensures they get notified directly and helps keep communication clear.*

Using Voice Typing & Add-ons

Google Docs offers voice typing and various add-ons to enhance your productivity:

1. **Voice Typing**:
   - o To use **Voice Typing**, go to **Tools > Voice typing**. Click on the microphone icon and start speaking—Google Docs will transcribe your words into text in real-time.

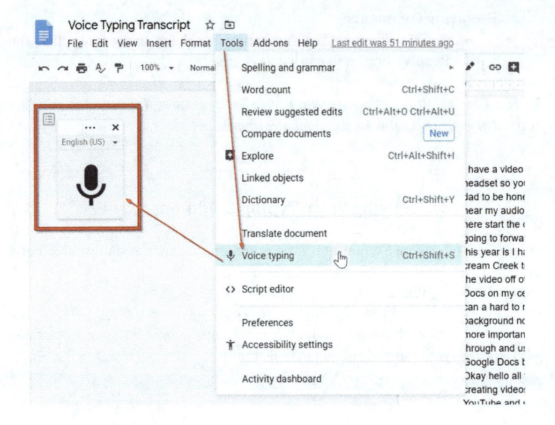

2. **Using Add-ons**:

    o Go to **Add-ons > Get add-ons** to browse and install a variety of tools that integrate with Google Docs, such as grammar checkers, citation generators, or productivity tools.

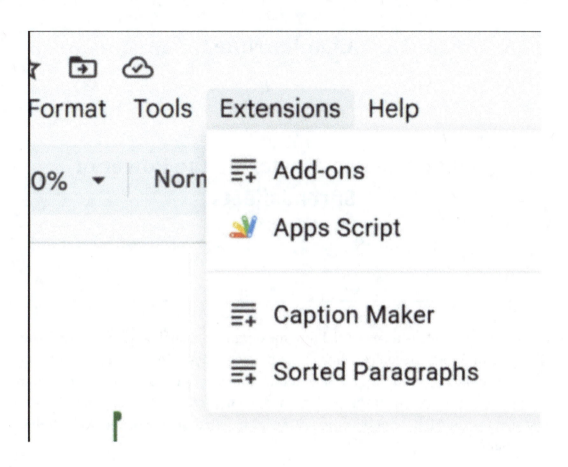

💡 *Tip: Voice typing can help you transcribe meetings, lectures, or brainstorm sessions quickly. Just make sure your microphone is working and clear of background noise.*

Conclusion

Google Docs provides everything you need to create professional and polished documents. From basic formatting to real-time collaboration, it's a versatile tool for individuals and teams. By mastering the features we've covered, you'll be able to create, edit, and share documents with ease. Whether you're writing a simple memo or a detailed report, Google Docs is your reliable platform for getting the job done efficiently.

Chapter Nine

Google Sheets – Mastering the Power of Spreadsheets

Google Sheets is an essential tool for organizing, analyzing, and visualizing data. Whether you're managing a budget, tracking inventory, or creating complex reports, Google Sheets offers a variety of tools and functions to make your spreadsheet tasks easier. In this chapter, we will explore the key features that will help you become proficient in using Google Sheets to its fullest potential.

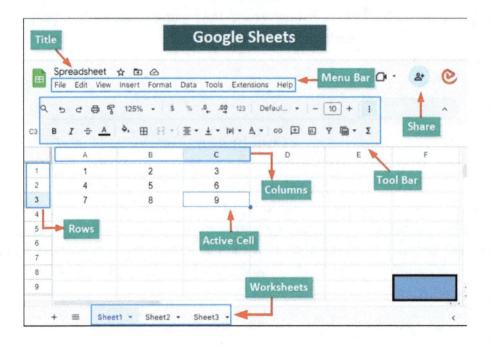

Basic Spreadsheet Navigation & Formatting

Before diving into formulas and data analysis, it's important to get familiar with navigating and formatting your Google Sheets:

1. **Navigating Sheets**:
   - The **Sheet tabs** at the bottom allow you to switch between different worksheets within a single file. You can rename, add, or delete sheets as needed.
2. **Cell Reference**:
   - Each cell in Google Sheets is referenced by a combination of column letters and row numbers, such as **A1**, **B2**, etc. You can click on cells to select them for editing.
3. **Basic Formatting**:
   - You can change the font, size, color, and alignment of your text using the **toolbar** at the top.

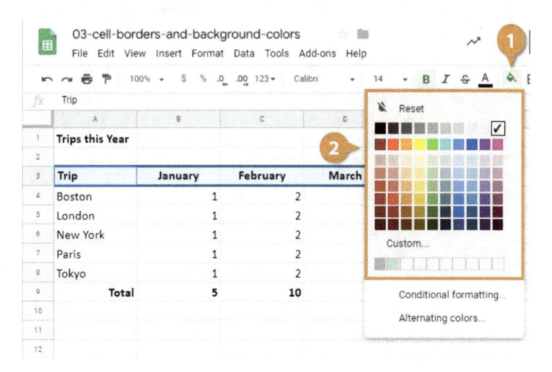

- Adjust column width and row height by clicking and dragging the borders.

💡 *Tip: Use **Freeze Rows/Columns** to keep headers or labels visible while scrolling through large spreadsheets. This option is under **View > Freeze**.*

Using Formulas & Functions (SUM, AVERAGE, VLOOKUP, etc.)

Google Sheets becomes even more powerful when you start using formulas and functions to calculate and manipulate data:

1. **Basic Functions**:
   - **SUM**: Adds up a range of numbers. Example: =SUM(A1:A10)

E5   fx   =SUM(E2:E4)

	A	B	C	D	E
1	Trainers	Pokeball	Great Balls	Ultra Balls	
2	Iva	2	3	1	6
3	Liam	5	5	2	12
4	Adora	10	2	3	15
5					=SUM(E2:E4)

E6   fx

	A	B	C	D	E
1	Trainers	Pokeball	Great Balls	Ultra Balls	
2	Iva	2	3	1	6
3	Liam	5	5	2	12
4	Adora	10	2	3	15
5					33
6					
7					

- **AVERAGE**: Calculates the average of a range. Example: =AVERAGE(B1:B10)
2. **Using VLOOKUP**:

- The **VLOOKUP** function helps you find data in large tables. It looks for a value in the first column and returns a corresponding value from another column. Example: =VLOOKUP(A2, A1:B10, 2, FALSE)
3. **Other Useful Functions**:
    - **COUNTIF**: Counts the number of cells that meet certain criteria. Example: =COUNTIF(C1:C10, ">50")
    - **IF**: Returns one value if a condition is true and another value if false. Example: =IF(A1>100, "Yes", "No")

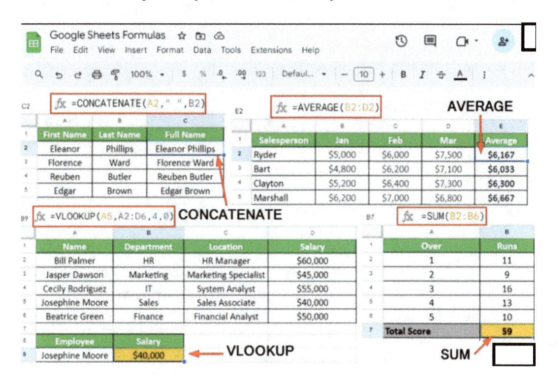

💡 *Tip: Google Sheets also supports more advanced functions like **INDEX/MATCH**, **QUERY**, and **IMPORTRANGE** to analyze large datasets across multiple sheets or files.*

Creating Charts & Graphs for Data Visualization

Data visualization helps you make sense of your data at a glance. Google Sheets provides several chart types to visualize trends and comparisons:

1. **Creating a Chart**:
   - Highlight the data you want to visualize, then click on **Insert > Chart**. Google Sheets will automatically suggest a chart type based on your data.

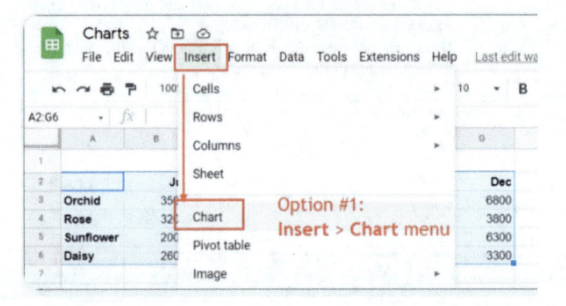

2. **Customizing Your Chart**:
   - Once the chart is inserted, you can modify the chart type, colors, axis labels, and more by clicking the **Chart editor** on the right.
3. **Types of Charts**:
   - Google Sheets offers various chart types, including **bar charts**, **line charts**, **pie charts**, and **scatter plots**.

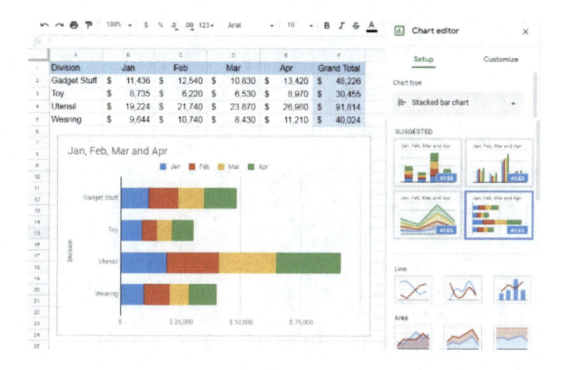

💡 *Tip: Use a **Combo Chart** to combine multiple chart types into one, which is helpful for displaying different datasets with varying units of measurement.*

Collaborating with Team Members in Google Sheets

Google Sheets excels in collaboration, allowing multiple people to work on the same document simultaneously:

1. **Sharing & Permissions**:
   o To share a sheet, click **Share** in the top right and set permissions (view, comment, or edit) for collaborators.

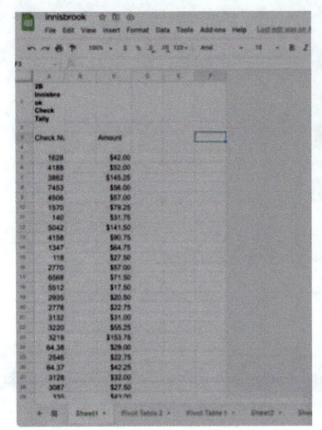

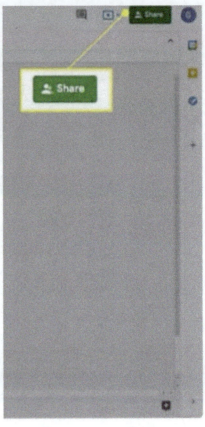

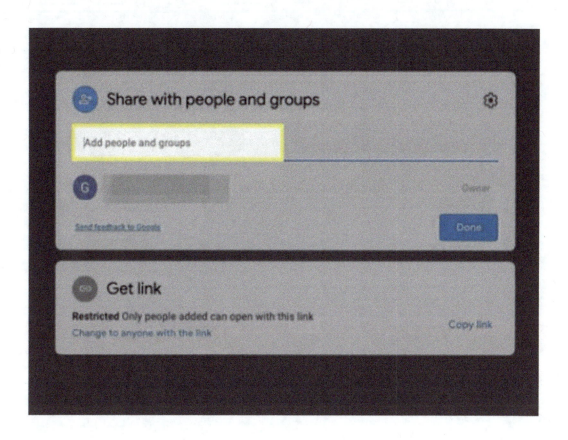

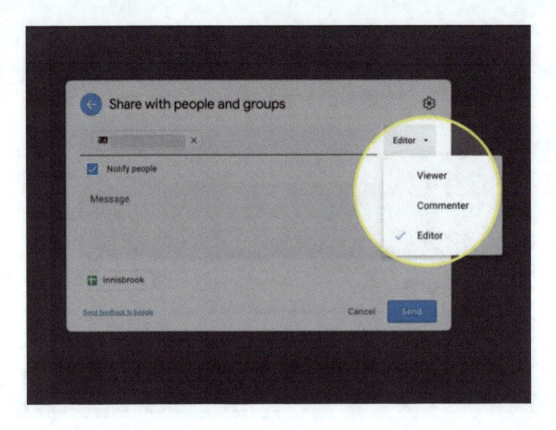

2. **Real-Time Collaboration**:
    o   As you and your team members edit the sheet, you'll see each other's changes in real-time. Each collaborator is identified by a different color.
3. **Commenting**:
    o   You can highlight a cell and click the **Add comment** button to leave feedback. Comments can be tagged with @mentions to notify specific team members. You can also right-click on a cell and select **comment.**

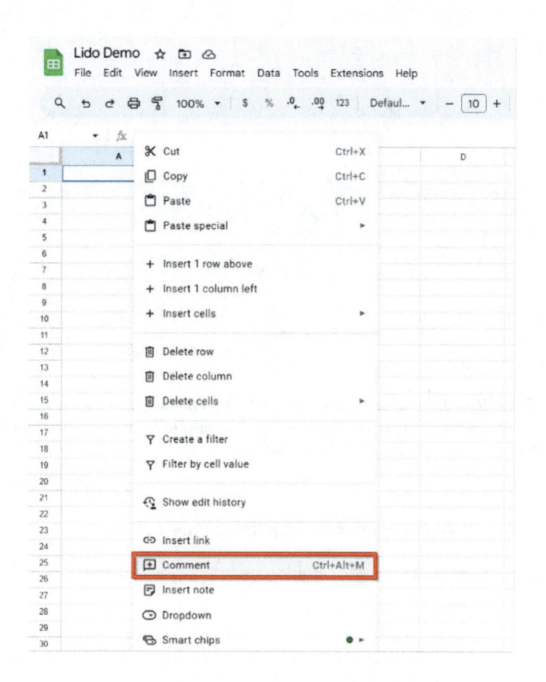

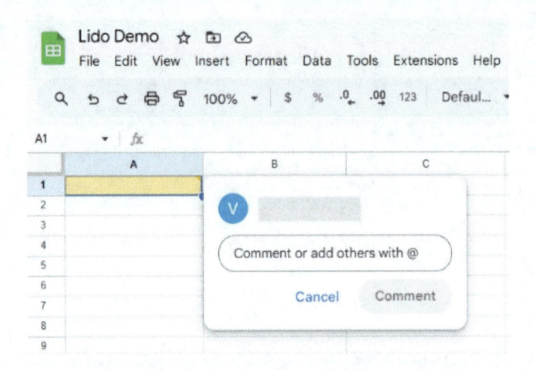

💡 *Tip: Use **Version History** (under **File > Version History**) to track and restore previous versions of the sheet. This is helpful if you need to revert back to an earlier version or check changes made by collaborators.*

Automating Tasks with Google Sheets Macros

Google Sheets allows you to automate repetitive tasks using **Macros**:

1. **Recording a Macro**:
   - To create a macro, go to **Extensions > Macros > Record Macro**. Perform the actions you want to automate, and then click **Save** when finished.

2. **Running a Macro**:
   o After saving your macro, you can run it anytime by going to **Extensions > Macros** and selecting the saved macro.
3. **Editing Macros**:
   o Macros are recorded in **Google Apps Script**, so you can open the **Script editor** (under **Extensions > Apps Script**) to modify or customize the macro code.

💡 *Tip: Use **Macros** for tasks like formatting, sorting data, or copying/pasting large sets of information to save time.*

Conclusion

Google Sheets is a powerful tool for managing, analyzing, and sharing data. Whether you're performing basic calculations or building complex data models, the tools and functions we've covered in this chapter will help you get the most out of your spreadsheet experience. By mastering the use of formulas, data visualization, and automation with macros, you can enhance your productivity and make data-driven decisions with ease.

Chapter Ten

Google Slides – Crafting Compelling Presentations

Google Slides is a versatile tool for creating and delivering presentations. Whether you're designing a pitch for a business meeting or creating an educational slideshow, Google Slides offers a range of features to help you design impactful presentations. In this chapter, we'll guide you through the essentials of creating and refining presentations that grab attention and convey your message clearly.

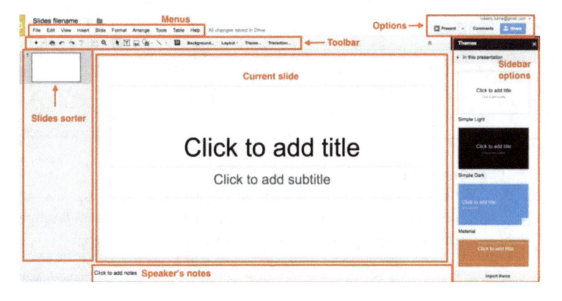

Creating a New Presentation from Scratch

To get started with Google Slides, follow these simple steps to create your presentation:

1. **Open Google Slides**:
   o Go to **slides.google.com** and click on **Blank** to start a new presentation from scratch, or select a **Template** to begin with a pre-designed layout.

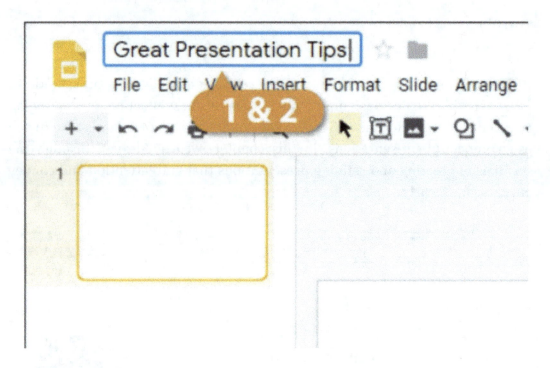

2. **Choosing a Theme**:
   o Google Slides offers a variety of themes that define the overall design of your presentation. To select one, click on **Slide > Change theme** and pick from the available options.

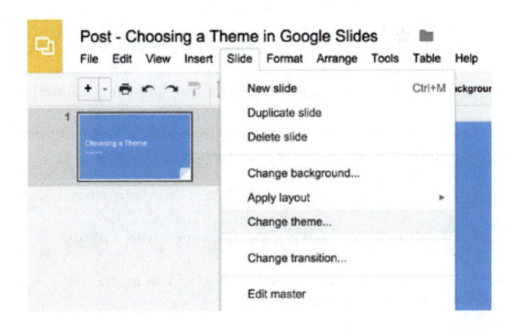

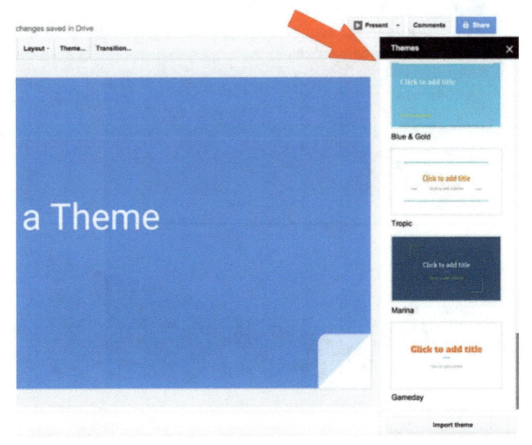

3. **Adding Slides**:
    o   To add a new slide, click on **+** on the toolbar or press **Ctrl + M** (Windows) or **Cmd + M** (Mac). You can select different slide layouts (e.g., title, content, etc.) to organize your presentation effectively.

💡 *Tip: Use **Master Slides** to set a consistent layout for all slides in your presentation. This feature helps with uniformity and ease of design.*

Adding & Formatting Text, Images, and Videos

Designing engaging slides requires incorporating various media. Here's how you can add and format these elements:

1. **Text**:
    o   Click on a text box to start typing. Use the toolbar at the top to adjust font size, style, and color.

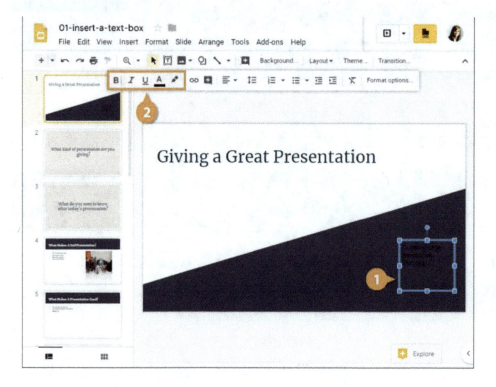

- To add a new text box, click on **Insert > Text box** and draw the box on the slide.

2. **Images**:
   - To insert images, click on **Insert > Image**, and choose from uploading from your computer, Google Drive, or using a URL.

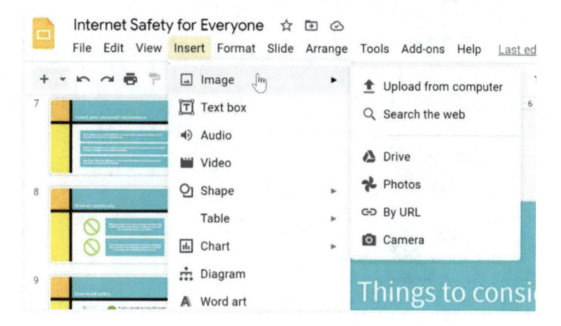

   - After inserting an image, you can resize, crop, and adjust the position.

3. **Videos**:
   - Insert videos by going to **Insert > Video**. You can add videos from YouTube or upload directly from your computer or Google Drive.

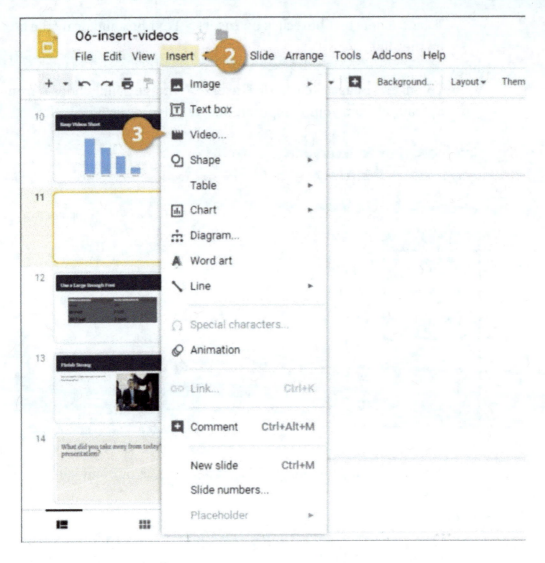

     o   Once added, you can resize and position the video within your slide.

💡 *Tip: To make your slides visually appealing, avoid clutter. Stick to a simple design with one key image and minimal text per slide.*

Applying Slide Transitions & Animations

Transitions and animations can bring your slides to life, making your presentation more dynamic:

1. **Slide Transitions**:
   - Click on **Slide > Transition** to apply transitions between slides. You can choose effects like **Fade**, **Slide**, or **Flip**.

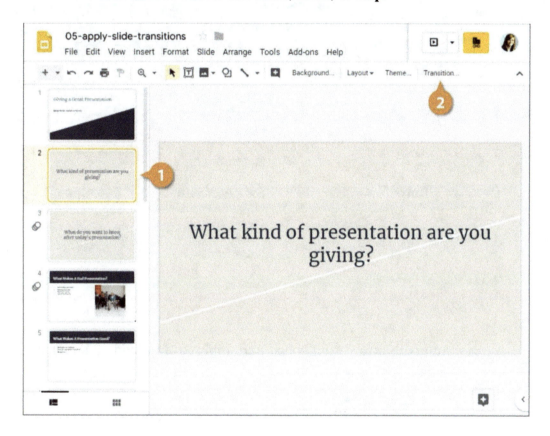

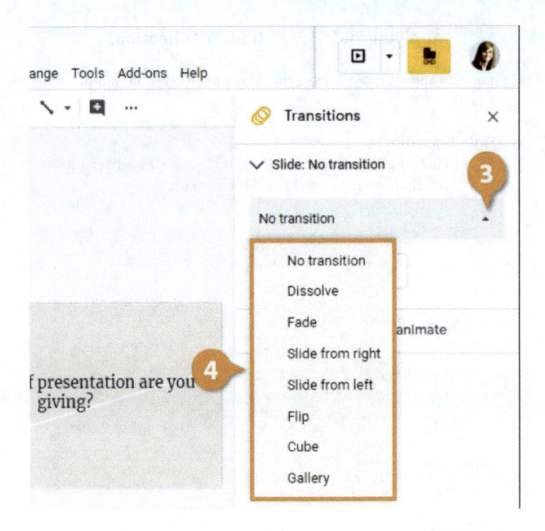

- o Adjust the transition speed and apply it to individual slides or all slides.

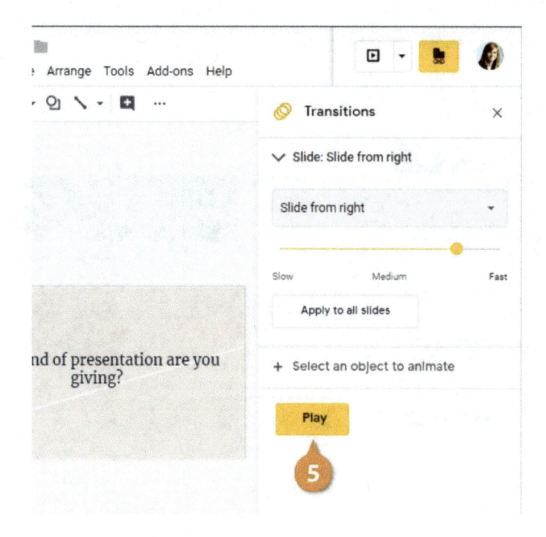

2. **Animations**:
    - Select a specific element (text box, image, etc.), click on **Insert > Animation**, and choose the type of animation you want (e.g., fade in, zoom in).

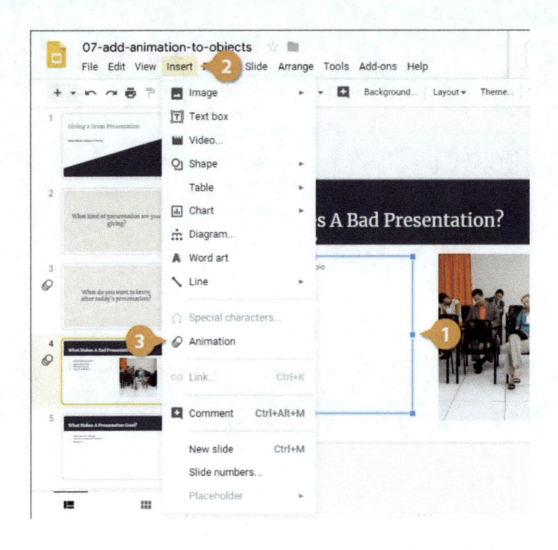

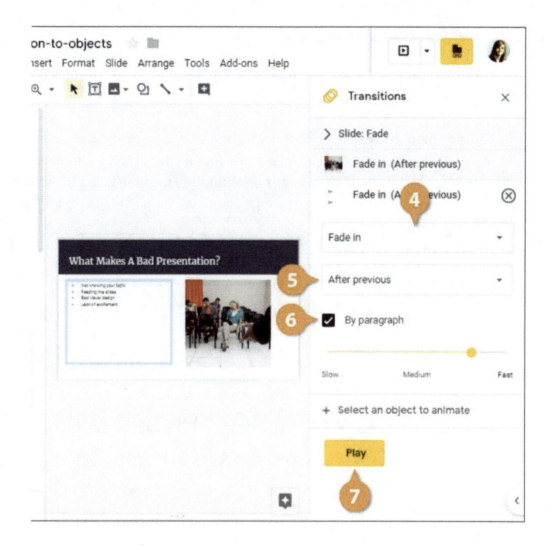

- o You can set the animation to start **on click**, **after previous**, or **with previous** to control the timing.

💡 *Tip: Keep transitions and animations simple to avoid distraction. Overuse of flashy effects can reduce the impact of your presentation.*

Presenting with Speaker Notes

Google Slides makes it easy to add speaker notes, helping you stay on track while presenting:

1. **Adding Speaker Notes**:
   - At the bottom of each slide, you'll find a space for **Speaker notes**. Here, you can add key points or reminders to guide you during your presentation.

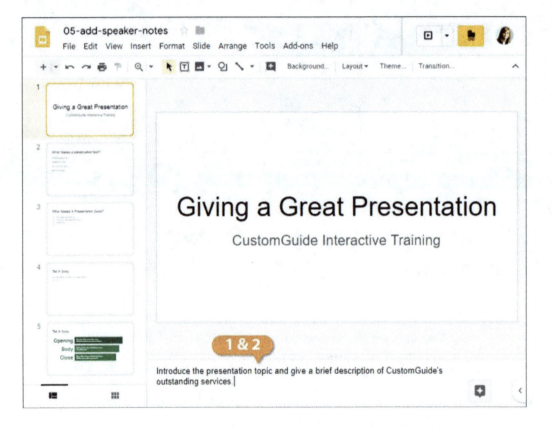

2. **Viewing Speaker Notes During the Presentation**:
   - To view your speaker notes while presenting, click on **Presenter view** in the top-right corner of the screen. This will show your slide, speaker notes, and a timer on your display.
3. **Printing or Sharing Notes**:

- You can print your speaker notes or save them as a PDF by going to **File > Print settings and preview > Notes pages**.

💡 *Tip: Use **speaker notes** to summarize your key points, but avoid reading directly from them. Use them as a guide to help you stay focused while engaging with your audience.*

Conclusion

With the tools provided by Google Slides, you can create presentations that are not only visually appealing but also effective in delivering your message. By mastering the features of text, images, transitions, and speaker notes, you can enhance the experience for your audience and ensure your ideas are communicated clearly and professionally. Whether you're preparing for a business presentation or a classroom lecture, Google Slides gives you the flexibility and functionality to present with confidence.

PART FOUR

Time & Task Management

Chapter Eleven

Google Calendar – Organizing Your Time Effectively

Google Calendar is a powerful tool for managing your schedule, whether for personal use or work-related events. It helps you stay on top of meetings, appointments, and important tasks by offering seamless integration with other Google Workspace tools. In this chapter, we will explore how to create, schedule, and manage events, set reminders, share calendars, and leverage Google Calendar's integrations with Gmail and Google Meet.

Creating & Scheduling Events

Google Calendar makes it easy to create events that fit your schedule. Here's how to create one:

1. **Creating a New Event**:
    o Open Google Calendar and click on **Create** in the top-left corner.

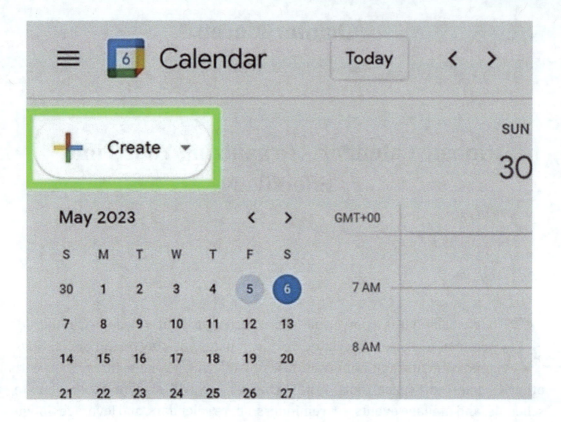

- You can also click on any open time slot in your calendar to create an event directly.
- In the pop-up window, enter the event details: title, date, time, location, and any additional information.

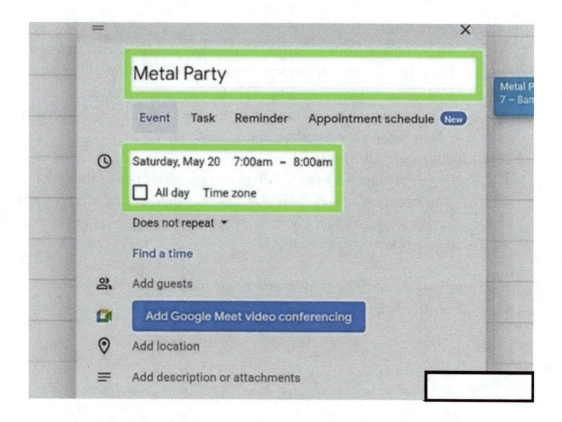

2. **Setting Event Details**:
   ○ Add a description of the event, if necessary, and select the relevant **event color** to help visually organize your schedule.
   ○ You can also set the event as **recurring** (daily, weekly, monthly) by selecting **Does not repeat** and choosing your preferred repeat settings.

💡 *Tip: Set event colors to categorize events by type (work, personal, etc.) to make your calendar visually organized.*

Setting Up Reminders & Notifications

Reminders and notifications ensure you never miss important events. Here's how you can set them up:

1. **Event Reminders**:
   ○ After creating your event, scroll down to the **Notification** section. You can set reminders by selecting **Add notification** and choosing a time (e.g., 10 minutes, 1 hour) before the event starts.
   ○ You can set multiple reminders for the same event (e.g., a reminder 1 hour before, and another 10 minutes before).
2. **Notifications for All Events**:
   ○ Go to **Settings > Event Settings** to set default notifications for all your events. You can choose the default notification time (e.g., 10 minutes before) and whether notifications appear via email or as pop-up alerts.

💡 *Tip: Set notifications for important meetings and appointments to help you stay on schedule. It's better to have a few reminders than to forget key events.*

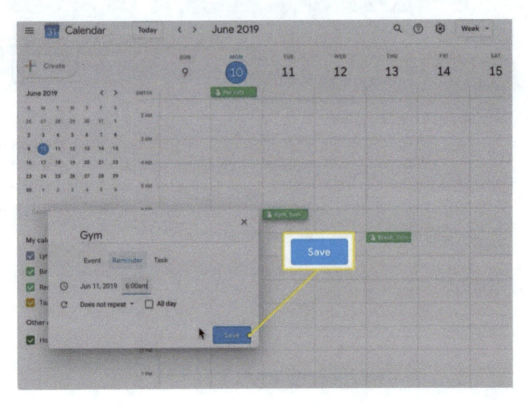

Sharing & Syncing Calendars with Others

Sharing your calendar can be a great way to coordinate with colleagues, family, or friends. Here's how to share and sync your Google Calendar:

1. **Sharing Your Calendar**:
   - In Google Calendar, find the calendar you want to share under **My calendars**. Hover over it, click the **three dots** icon, and select **Settings and sharing**.

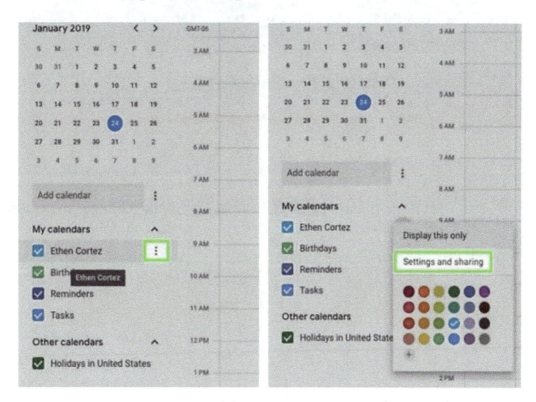

   - Under **Share with specific people**, add the email addresses of the people you want to share your calendar with.

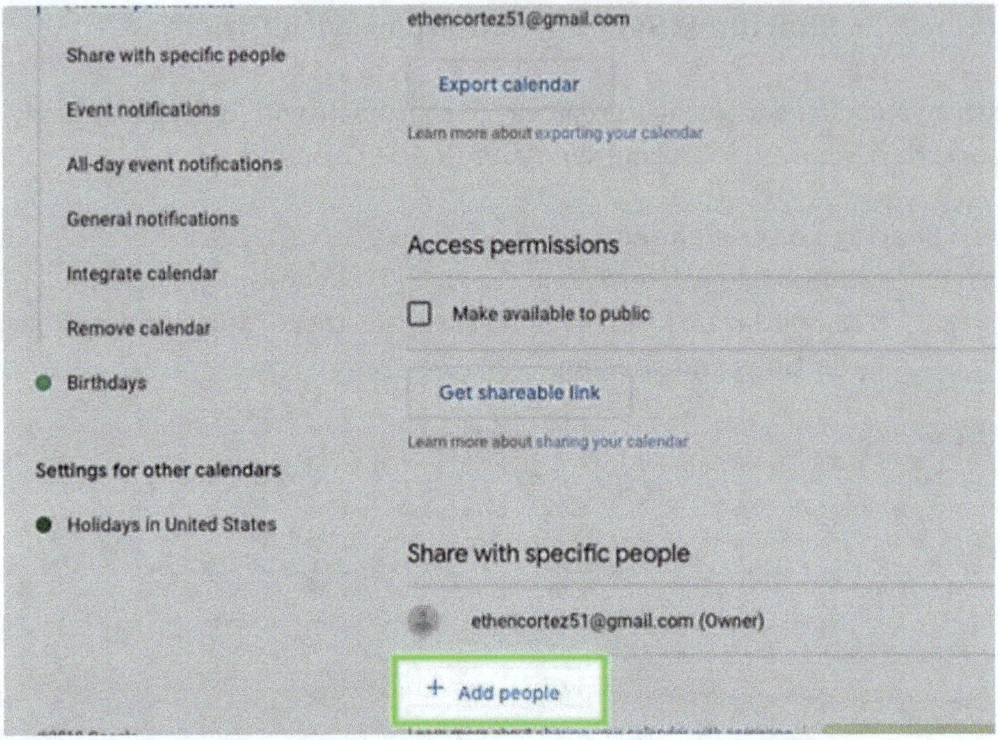

Share with specific people
Event notifications
All-day event notifications
General notifications
Integrate calendar
Remove calendar
● Birthdays

Settings for other calendars

● Holidays in United States

ethencortez51@gmail.com

Export calendar

Learn more about exporting your calendar

Access permissions

☐ Make available to public

Get shareable link

Learn more about sharing your calendar

Share with specific people

ethencortez51@gmail.com (Owner)

+ Add people

- ○ Set the permission level (e.g., **View only**, **Make changes to events**) for each person.

2. **Syncing with Other Calendars**:
   - Google Calendar allows you to sync with calendars from other services, such as Outlook or Apple Calendar. Go to **Settings > Add calendar** and follow the prompts to add external calendars.

💡 *Tip: Use shared calendars for team or family events to ensure everyone stays informed and up to date.*

Using Google Calendar with Gmail & Google Meet

Google Calendar integrates seamlessly with Gmail and Google Meet, offering additional functionality and efficiency:

1. **Creating Events from Gmail**:
   - If you receive an email about an event or appointment in Gmail, you can automatically add it to Google Calendar. Google will often detect event details like date and time in emails.
   - To add it to your calendar, click the **Add to Calendar** button found in the email.
2. **Scheduling Google Meet Calls**:
   - When creating an event in Google Calendar, you can easily add a **Google Meet link** to the event by selecting **Add Google Meet video conferencing**. This generates a unique meeting link that participants can join with just a click.

💡 *Tip: Use **Google Meet** for virtual meetings directly from Google Calendar. It ensures everyone has the meeting link and can join with ease.*

Conclusion

Google Calendar is a highly effective tool for managing your appointments, reminders, and events. By learning to create and schedule events, set reminders, share calendars, and integrate it with Gmail and Google Meet, you'll maximize your productivity and stay organized. Whether it's for personal use, team coordination, or scheduling virtual meetings, Google Calendar helps streamline your time management.

Chapter Twelve

Google Keep – Efficient Note-Taking & Idea Organization

Google Keep is a versatile tool for capturing ideas, organizing notes, and setting reminders. With its simple and user-friendly interface, it's perfect for both personal use and work-related tasks. In this chapter, we'll explore how to create and format notes, organize them with labels and color codes, set reminders, and ensure your notes are always accessible by syncing them across devices.

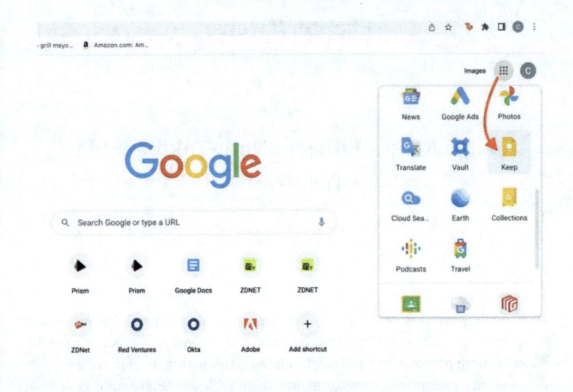

This is how to find Google Keep in your G Suite

Creating & Formatting Notes

Google Keep allows you to quickly jot down ideas, tasks, or to-do lists. Here's how to create and format notes:

1. **Creating a New Note**:
   - Open **Google Keep** from your browser or mobile device.
   - To create a new note, click the **Take a note** section at the top or the **+** icon on mobile.

- Type your note content, add images, or even record audio notes by clicking the appropriate icons.

2. **Formatting Notes**:
   - Google Keep doesn't offer advanced formatting options, but you can make simple changes to your text. You can use checkboxes for to-do lists or add bullet points to organize ideas.
   - You can also use **voice input** to dictate your notes hands-free.

💡 *Tip: Use the checkboxes feature for to-do lists, and tick them off as you complete tasks. It keeps your ideas and actions organized and actionable.*

Using Labels & Color Codes for Organization

To keep your notes organized, Google Keep lets you apply labels and color codes. Here's how to manage them:

1. **Adding Labels**:
   - To apply a label, open the note and click the **three dots** icon (More options) at the bottom-right corner.
   - Select **Add label** and create a new label or choose an existing one. Labels are helpful for grouping related notes (e.g., "Work", "Personal", "Ideas").

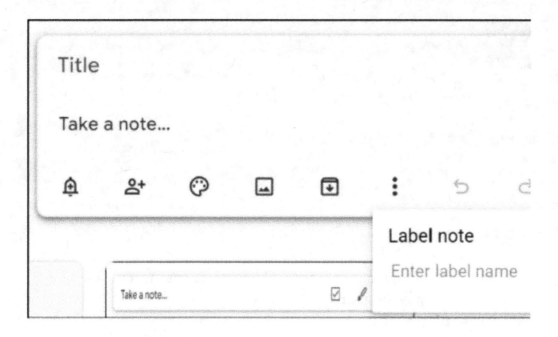

2. **Color Coding Notes**:
   - You can color-code your notes for quick identification. To do so, open a note, click the **three dots** icon, and select **Change color**.
   - Choose from a variety of colors to visually categorize your notes, making it easier to locate them later.

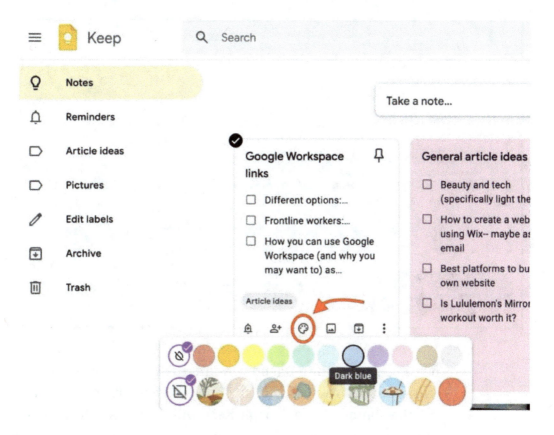

💡 *Tip: Use color coding for different categories (e.g., blue for work, green for personal) to create a visually organized system.*

Setting Reminders & Syncing Across Devices

Google Keep makes it easy to stay on track with your tasks and ideas by offering reminder features. You can also sync your notes across multiple devices for easy access wherever you are.

1. **Setting Reminders**:
   o Open a note and click the **bell icon** at the bottom of the note to set a reminder.

- You can choose a **time-based reminder** (e.g., at a specific time) or **location-based reminder** (e.g., when you arrive at a certain place).
- Once the reminder is set, Google Keep will notify you when the time or location is reached.

2. **Syncing Across Devices**:
   - Google Keep syncs automatically across all devices where you're signed into your Google account. Whether you're on your phone, tablet, or computer, your notes stay updated.
   - Simply open the Google Keep app or website on any device to access your notes in real-time.

💡 *Tip: Set location-based reminders for tasks that need to be done when you reach a specific place (e.g., "Remind me to call the client when I arrive at the office").*

Conclusion

Google Keep is a simple yet effective tool for organizing your ideas, tasks, and notes. By creating and formatting notes, applying labels and color codes, setting reminders, and syncing across devices, you can ensure that your thoughts are organized and easily accessible at all times. Whether it's for quick reminders or detailed notes, Google Keep offers an efficient way to capture and manage your ideas.

Chapter Thirteen

Google Tasks – Efficient To-Do List Management

G oogle Tasks is an excellent tool for keeping track of your to-dos, from simple daily tasks to more detailed project steps. It integrates seamlessly with Gmail and Google Calendar, making it easier to stay on top of your commitments. In this chapter, we'll dive into how to create and manage tasks and subtasks, link tasks with Gmail and Google Calendar, and set deadlines and reminders to ensure nothing slips through the cracks.

Creating Tasks & Subtasks

Google Tasks allows you to create simple to-do lists with the option to break tasks into smaller, manageable subtasks. Here's how to organize your tasks effectively:

1. **Creating a Task**:
    - Open **Google Tasks** via the sidebar in Gmail or Google Calendar, or directly from the Google Tasks app.

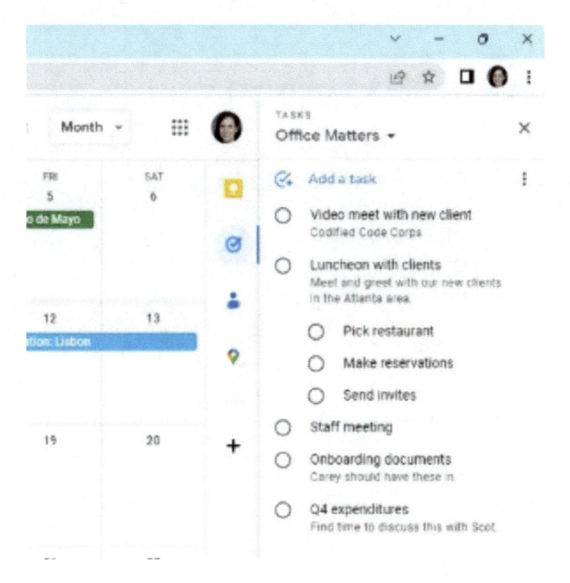

- o Click the **+ Add a task** button to create a new task. Enter a title for the task, and optionally, add details or notes for clarity.

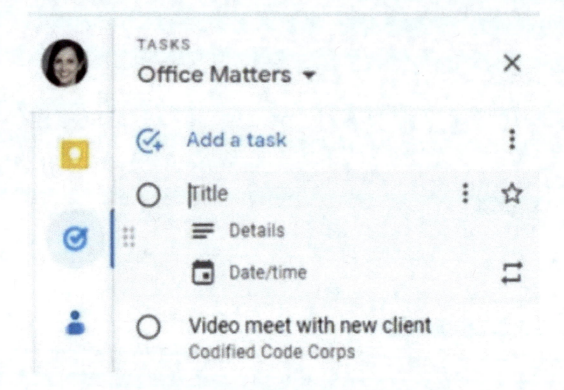

2. **Adding Subtasks**:
   o Once you've created a task, click the **three dots** next to it and select **Add a subtask**.

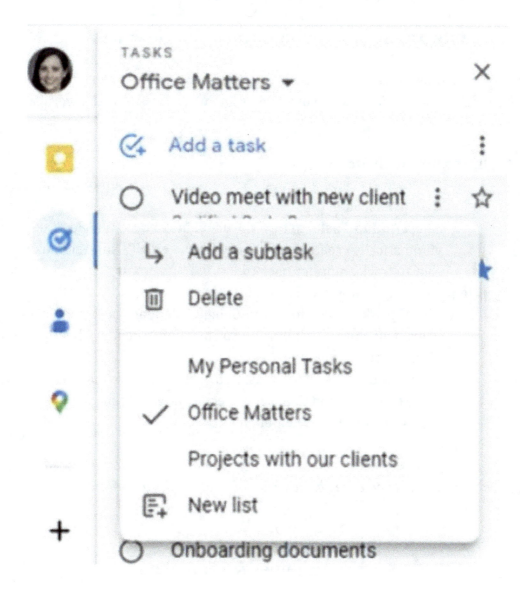

     o   Add subtasks for more detailed steps related to the main task. This is helpful for larger tasks that require several smaller actions.

💡 *Tip: Break large tasks into smaller subtasks for a more structured approach. For example, a task like "Prepare Report" can have subtasks like "Research data," "Draft introduction," and "Proofread."

Integrating Tasks with Gmail & Google Calendar

Google Tasks integrates smoothly with both Gmail and Google Calendar, ensuring that your tasks stay in sync with your daily schedule. Here's how to leverage this integration:

1. **Integrating with Gmail**:
   - When you receive an email that requires follow-up or action, click the **Tasks** icon in Gmail.
   - Select **Add to Tasks** to turn the email into a task. Google Tasks will automatically create a new task with the email's subject, making it easy to track and refer back to.
2. **Integrating with Google Calendar**:
   - Google Tasks is also linked to Google Calendar. Tasks with set due dates will automatically appear in your calendar, helping you visualize your schedule.
   - To set a due date for a task, click on the task and select **Add date/time**. You can then set a specific date and time for the task to appear in your Google Calendar.

💡 *Tip: Turn important emails into tasks by clicking the "Add to Tasks" option. It helps you avoid forgetting time-sensitive actions hidden in your inbox.*

Setting Deadlines & Reminders

Google Tasks allows you to set deadlines and reminders, ensuring that you stay on track and complete your tasks on time. Here's how to set them:

1. **Setting Deadlines**:
   - Open a task and click the **Add date/time** option. You can choose a specific date and time for the task to be due.
   - Once the due date is set, the task will appear in your Google Calendar, making it easy to visualize your deadlines.
2. **Setting Reminders**:

o   While Google Tasks does not have a built-in reminder function like Google Calendar, it will send you a notification when the task is due if it's linked with your calendar. You can also set a time for a notification to pop up.

💡 *Tip: Use due dates in Google Tasks to sync your to-dos with your calendar and set up reminders for important tasks to make sure you never miss a deadline.*

Conclusion

Google Tasks is a simple yet powerful tool for managing your to-do lists, whether you're working on a personal project or keeping track of work-related tasks. By creating tasks and subtasks, integrating with Gmail and Google Calendar, and setting deadlines and reminders, you can stay organized and on top of everything you need to do.

PART FIVE

Business & Team Tools

Chapter Fourteen

Google Sites – Building Websites Without Code

G oogle Sites offers a simple, intuitive way to create websites without the need for any coding skills. Whether you need a personal portfolio, a team collaboration site, or a project hub, Google Sites provides the tools to easily bring your ideas to life. In this chapter, we'll walk through the process of creating a website, customizing layouts, adding pages, and managing permissions to ensure your site is tailored to your needs.

Creating a Website Using Google Sites

Creating a website with Google Sites is straightforward, even for beginners. Here's how to get started:

1. **Access Google Sites**:
   - Go to Google Sites and sign in with your Google account.
   - Click on **Blank** to start a new site from scratch, or choose from various templates for specific website types like portfolios or project sites.

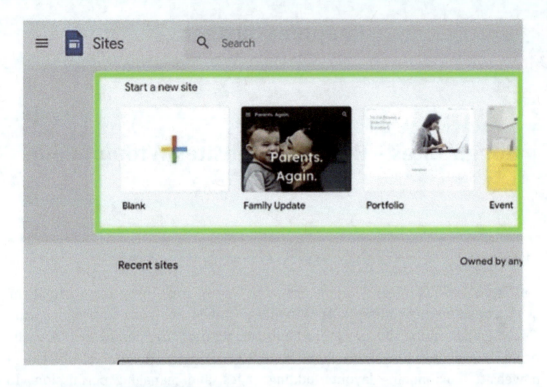

2. **Choosing a Template**:
   - Google Sites offers a variety of pre-made templates designed for different purposes. Select the one that best fits your needs, or start from a blank canvas if you prefer complete customization.

3. **Editing the Site**:
   - Once you've chosen a template or started with a blank page, you can begin editing. Google Sites has a drag-and-drop interface, making it easy to add content and adjust the layout without coding.

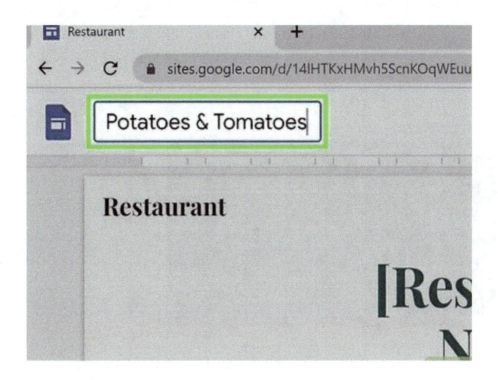

Enter your Site name

💡 *Tip: Take your time exploring the templates to find one that suits your purpose. Templates often include well-designed features, such as contact forms or navigation menus, that can save you time.*

Customizing Layouts & Adding Pages

After setting up your website, the next step is to customize the layout and add content. Google Sites makes this process simple:

1. **Customizing the Layout**:
   - To modify the layout of your site, click on the **Themes** option in the right-hand sidebar. You can choose from different themes to give your site a professional look.

- Use the **Insert** menu to add elements like text boxes, images, videos, calendars, and maps. The layout can be adjusted by dragging these elements around the page.

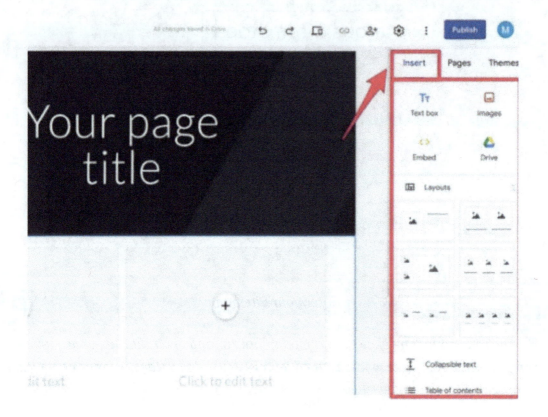

- Customize the color scheme and fonts to align with your brand or style.

2. **Adding Pages**:
   - To add additional pages to your site, click the **Pages** tab on the right and select **+**. You can create multiple pages, such as an About page, Contact page, or Blog.

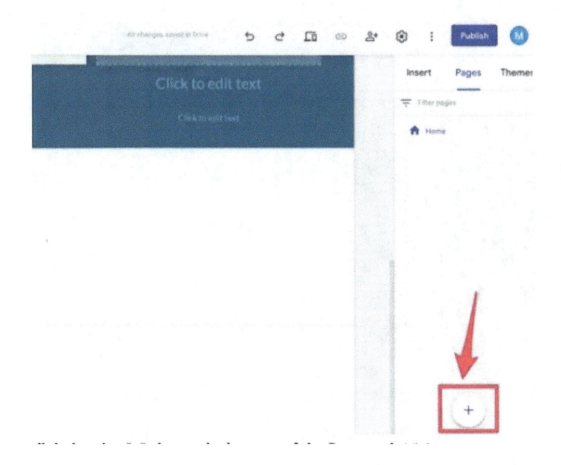

    ○ Arrange the pages in a logical order using the navigation menu. The site structure is automatically updated as you add new pages.

💡 *Tip: Organize your site with a clean and intuitive menu. Ensure that the most important pages, such as "About" or "Contact," are easy to find for visitors.*

Publishing & Managing Permissions

Once your website is ready, it's time to publish and control who can view or edit your site. Here's how to manage permissions and publish your website:

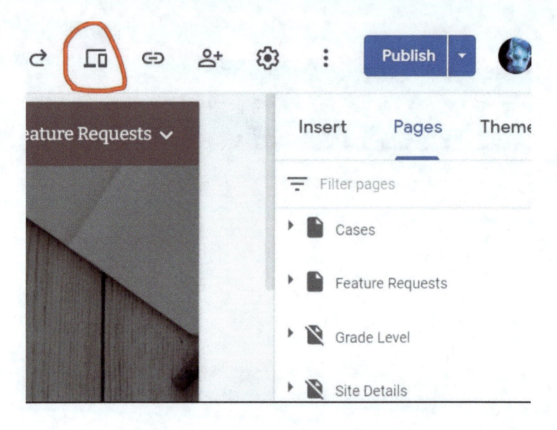

Click the Preview button to see how the site will look like

1. **Publishing the Site**:
   - When you're happy with your site, click the **Publish** button in the top right corner. You'll be prompted to choose a custom URL for your website (e.g., sites.google.com/view/yourwebsite).

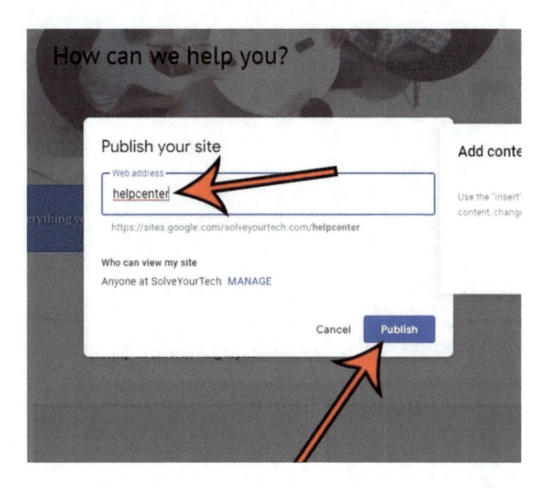

- If you prefer a custom domain, you can link your Google Sites to a domain you own.

2. **Managing Permissions**:
   - After publishing, you can control who has access to your website. Click **Share with others** to add editors or collaborators. You can give people permission to either view or edit the site.

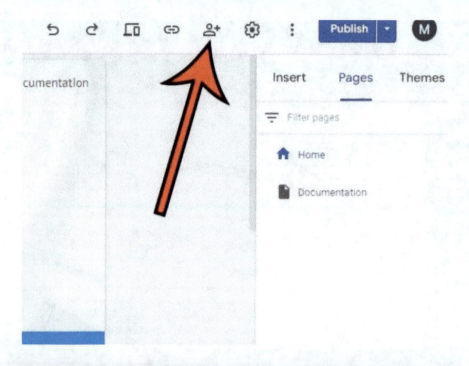

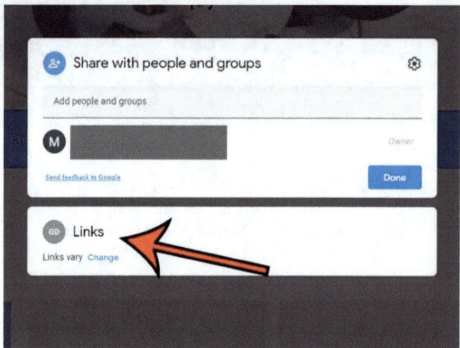

  o For private sites, set permissions so that only specific people can view or edit the content.

💡 *Tip: Before publishing your site, review all the content for errors, and make sure all links and images are working properly. Consider testing the site with a small group of people to get feedback before going live.*

Conclusion

Google Sites provides a user-friendly platform for building websites without requiring any coding knowledge. Whether you're building a personal site, a team collaboration space, or an event page, Google Sites gives you the flexibility and ease of use to create a professional website quickly.

With the ability to customize layouts, add pages, and manage permissions, you can create a website that fits your needs and is easy to maintain. Publish your site with confidence, knowing you can manage who sees and edits your content.

Chapter Fifteen

Google Admin Console – Efficiently Managing Google Workspace for Your Business

The Google Admin Console is the central hub for managing your organization's Google Workspace settings. It gives you complete control over users, roles, and security settings, ensuring a smooth and secure operation of your business's digital tools. This chapter will guide you through adding and managing users, assigning roles and permissions, and monitoring security and compliance to maintain a safe environment.

Adding & Managing Users

Managing users is a crucial part of the Admin Console, as it allows you to control who has access to your organization's resources.

1. **Adding New Users**:
   - From the Admin Console dashboard, click on **Users** and then the **Add New User** button.

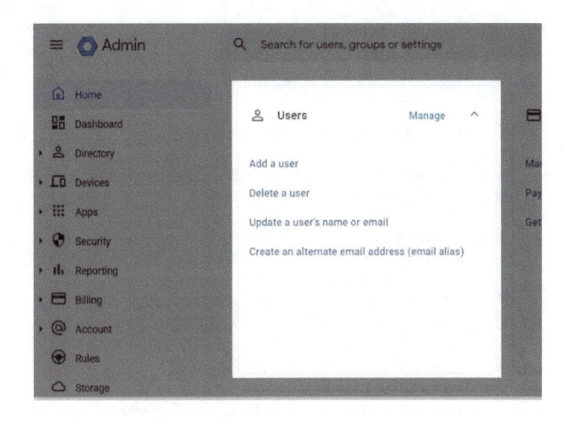

- Enter the necessary details for the new user, including name, email address, and any other required information.
- After adding the user, you can assign them a custom email address and provide them with access to specific Google Workspace services based on your company's needs.

2. **Managing User Accounts**:
   - You can edit user details, change passwords, and update access levels from the user management section.
   - If an employee leaves the organization, you can deactivate their account, ensuring that sensitive company information remains secure.
   - You can also organize users into **organizational units** to group them based on departments or teams, allowing you to apply customized settings for different groups of users.

Tip: Regularly review user access and deactivate accounts for former employees promptly to maintain security.

Assigning Roles & Permissions

Roles and permissions allow you to define the level of access that different users have within Google Workspace.

1. **Assigning Roles**:
   - From the Admin Console, go to **Roles** to create or assign roles to users. Google Workspace provides predefined roles such as Admin, User, and Groups Admin, or you can create custom roles.
   - Assign the appropriate role based on the user's responsibilities. For example, an Admin has full access to all settings, while a User may only have access to basic tools like Gmail and Google Drive.
2. **Permissions Management**:
   - Customize permissions for each role to control what users can and cannot do within your Google Workspace environment.
   - You can grant or restrict access to certain services, such as Google Meet or Google Docs, ensuring that users only have access to the tools they need for their work.

Tip: Be cautious when assigning Admin roles. Only grant this access to trusted individuals as it gives them control over all aspects of Google Workspace.

Monitoring Security & Compliance

Google Workspace provides comprehensive security and compliance monitoring tools to help you protect your organization's data and comply with regulations.

1. **Security Dashboard**:

- The **Security Dashboard** in the Admin Console allows you to monitor potential security threats, such as suspicious login attempts or unauthorized access to files.
- You can configure alerts to be notified if there are any unusual activities that may compromise your organization's security.

2. **Audit Logs**:
   - Use **Audit Logs** to review user activity and changes made within Google Workspace. This can help you track actions like file sharing, login attempts, and settings changes.
   - Regularly review these logs to ensure that no unauthorized actions are taking place within your organization.

3. **Compliance Settings**:
   - Google Workspace helps you maintain compliance with various regulations by providing features like **Data Loss Prevention (DLP)**, **eDiscovery**, and **Retention Rules** for emails and files.
   - These tools help ensure that sensitive information is protected and that your company adheres to necessary legal requirements.

💡 *Tip: Enable 2FA (Two-Factor Authentication) for all users to further strengthen the security of your Google Workspace environment.*

Conclusion

The Google Admin Console is an essential tool for managing your organization's Google Workspace environment. By effectively adding and managing users, assigning roles and permissions, and monitoring security and compliance, you can maintain a secure and efficient system that enhances productivity while protecting your organization's data.

With its user-friendly interface and comprehensive management tools, the Admin Console ensures that you have full control over your business's digital workspace, enabling your team to work securely and efficiently.

PART SIX

Automation & Advanced Features

Chapter Sixteen

Google Apps Script – Automating Google Workspace Tasks

G oogle Apps Script is a powerful tool that enables you to automate tasks and enhance the functionality of Google Workspace applications, such as Google Docs, Sheets, Gmail, and more. This chapter introduces you to Google Apps Script and demonstrates how to write scripts that streamline your workflow, create custom add-ons, and automate repetitive tasks.

Introduction to Google Apps Script

Google Apps Script is a JavaScript-based platform that allows you to write custom scripts to automate processes within Google Workspace apps. It provides a rich set of APIs that allow interaction with Google services like Gmail, Drive, Docs, Sheets, Calendar, and more.

- **Where to Start**:
  - To access Google Apps Script, open any Google Workspace app (e.g., Google Sheets) and navigate to **Extensions > Apps Script**. This will open the script editor where you can write and run your code.

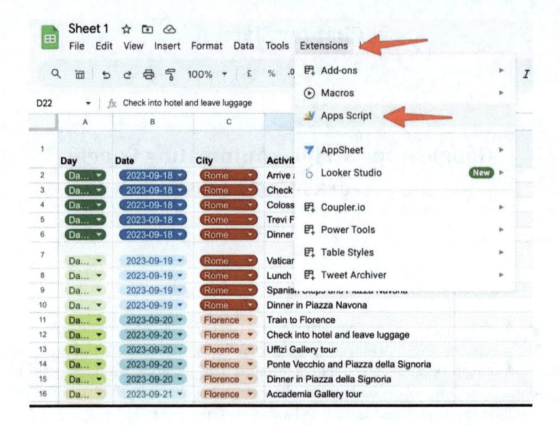

- **How It Works**:
  - Google Apps Script allows you to extend the built-in functionality of Google Workspace applications. For example, you can use it to send automated emails, update spreadsheets, create custom workflows, and integrate with third-party applications.

💡 *Tip: Familiarize yourself with the Google Apps Script documentation to understand available classes and methods that can be used in your scripts.*

Writing Basic Scripts to Automate Tasks

Once you understand the basics of Google Apps Script, you can start automating common tasks that can save time and effort.

1. **Automating Gmail**:

o   You can write scripts to automatically send emails, filter messages, or label emails. For example, the following script sends a simple email:

```
function sendEmail() {
  MailApp.sendEmail('recipient@example.com', 'Subject', 'Message body');
}
```

2. **Automating Google Sheets**:

- Google Sheets can be easily automated using Google Apps Script. For example, you can write a script that populates data into a spreadsheet or performs calculations:

```
function addDataToSheet() {
  var sheet = SpreadsheetApp.getActiveSpreadsheet().getActiveSheet();
  sheet.appendRow(['John', 'Doe', 'john@example.com']);
}
```

3. **Scheduling Scripts to Run Automatically**:
   o   Apps Script allows you to set triggers to run scripts at specified intervals, such as sending a weekly email or updating a document every day. This can be done by using **Time-driven triggers**.

💡 *Tip: Use the "Run" button in the Apps Script editor to test and debug your scripts before automating them.*

Creating Custom Google Docs & Sheets Add-ons

One of the most powerful features of Google Apps Script is the ability to create custom add-ons for Google Docs and Sheets. These add-ons can enhance the functionality of the apps and allow you to create personalized tools for your organization.

1. **Creating a Google Docs Add-on**:
    - You can create a custom menu in Google Docs to add new functionality. For example, the following script creates a custom menu that allows you to insert a specific piece of text into your document:

```
function onOpen() {
  var ui = DocumentApp.getUi();
  ui.createMenu('Custom Menu')
    .addItem('Insert Text', 'insertText')
    .addToUi();
}

function insertText() {
  var body = DocumentApp.getActiveDocument().getBody();
  body.appendParagraph('This is a custom text inserted by Apps Script.');
}
```

2. **Creating a Google Sheets Add-on**:

- In Google Sheets, you can build a custom sidebar or dialog box to interact with users. For example, a script could provide an input form that populates a spreadsheet based on user input:

```
function showSidebar() {
  var html = HtmlService.createHtmlOutputFromFile('form.html')
    .setTitle('Custom Form')
    .setWidth(300);
  SpreadsheetApp.getUi().showSidebar(html);
}
```

3. **Publishing Your Add-ons**:

   ○ Once you've created your add-ons, you can publish them in the Google Workspace Marketplace so that others can use them. This allows you to share your custom tools with colleagues or even the wider public.

💡 *Tip: When creating add-ons, ensure they are user-friendly by providing clear instructions and intuitive interfaces.*

Conclusion

Google Apps Script offers vast potential for automating tasks and creating custom workflows within Google Workspace. Whether you want to automate repetitive tasks, integrate external services, or develop custom add-ons, Apps Script can enhance productivity and streamline your processes. By learning how to write basic scripts and build custom add-ons, you'll be able to tailor Google Workspace to better fit your unique needs

Chapter Seventeen

Google Workspace Integrations & Enhancing Productivity with Third-Party Apps

G oogle Workspace is a powerful suite of tools on its own, but when combined with third-party applications, it can become even more efficient and customizable. This chapter explores how to integrate Google Workspace with popular apps like Zapier, Slack, Trello, Asana, and Chrome extensions to enhance your productivity and streamline your workflows.

Connecting Google Workspace with Zapier

Zapier is an online automation tool that connects your favorite apps and automates repetitive tasks without requiring coding. With Google Workspace integrated into Zapier, you can automate various workflows between Google Workspace apps and thousands of other apps.

- **What is Zapier?**
    - Zapier allows you to create "Zaps," which are automated workflows between apps. For example, you can set up a Zap to automatically save Gmail attachments to Google Drive or create a new Google Calendar event when you receive an email with a certain subject line.
- **Setting Up a Zap**:

- To connect Google Workspace with Zapier:
    1. Sign up for a Zapier account.
    2. Choose Google Workspace apps (e.g., Gmail, Google Sheets) as triggers and other apps (e.g., Slack, Trello) as actions.

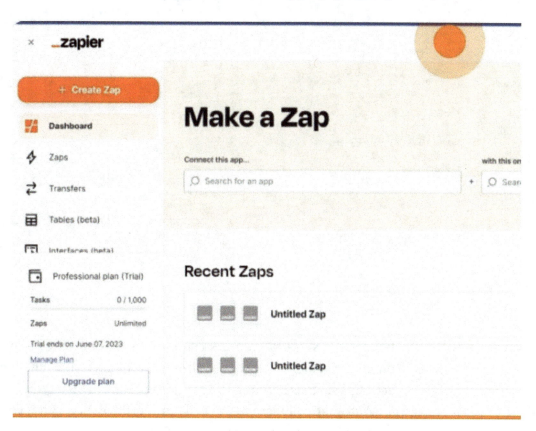

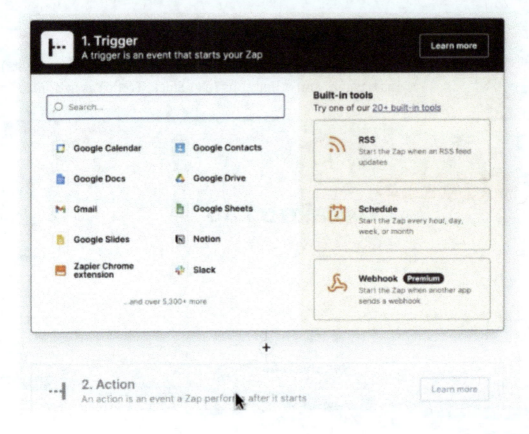

3. Follow the step-by-step instructions to connect both apps, define triggers (like receiving a new email), and choose actions (such as sending the email's content to Slack).
   o Example: Automatically create a task in Trello every time you receive an email marked as important in Gmail.

💡 *Tip: Explore popular pre-built Zaps in Zapier's app directory to quickly get started.*

Using Google Workspace with Slack, Trello & Asana

Integrating Google Workspace with collaboration and project management tools like Slack, Trello, and Asana can significantly enhance team productivity. Here's how these integrations work:

1. **Slack Integration**:
    - Slack is a messaging app that facilitates team communication. By integrating Slack with Google Workspace, you can streamline communication and increase efficiency.
        - **Examples of Integration**:
            - **Google Drive**: Share Google Drive files directly within Slack channels and receive notifications when files are updated.
            - **Google Calendar**: Get reminders in Slack for upcoming events or meetings.
            - **Gmail**: Send emails or share Gmail messages directly into Slack channels.
    - **Setting Up**: Install the Slack integration for Google Workspace through the Google Workspace Marketplace or Slack's app directory and follow the instructions to link your accounts.
2. **Trello Integration**:
    - Trello is a project management tool that uses boards and cards to organize tasks. By integrating Google Workspace, you can enhance project management within your team.
        - **Examples of Integration**:
            - **Google Calendar**: Sync Google Calendar with Trello to create due dates and track deadlines for tasks.
            - **Google Drive**: Attach Google Drive documents to Trello cards for easy access.
    - **Setting Up**: Install the Trello Power-Up for Google Workspace from the Trello board, which will allow you to attach files from Google Drive or link calendar events.
3. **Asana Integration**:
    - Asana is another popular project management tool that helps teams organize and track work. With Google Workspace integration, you can manage tasks and share documents more effectively.
        - **Examples of Integration**:
            - **Google Drive**: Attach Google Drive files to tasks in Asana.

- **Gmail**: Convert emails into tasks within Asana to track and manage projects.
  - ○ **Setting Up**: Add the Google Workspace integration to Asana through the Asana app directory and connect your Google Workspace apps with your Asana account.

💡 *Tip: Integrating Google Workspace with these tools can help streamline project management and communication, saving time and reducing the need for manual updates.*

Enhancing Productivity with Chrome Extensions

Google Chrome extensions are small tools that enhance the functionality of your browser. When used with Google Workspace, they can improve your workflow, add new features, and save you time.

1. **Google Workspace Extensions**:
   - ○ **Google Docs & Sheets**: Extensions like **Grammarly** can help you proofread and edit your documents in Google Docs, while **DocuSign** allows you to electronically sign documents directly within Google Docs or Sheets.
   - ○ **Google Meet**: Extensions like **Google Meet Enhancement Suite** add extra features to Google Meet, such as screen recording, background blur, and more.
2. **Productivity Extensions**:
   - ○ **Trello**: The Trello Chrome extension allows you to quickly add websites or tasks from your browser to your Trello board.
   - ○ **Slack**: The Slack extension enables you to easily share webpages and communicate with your team directly through your browser.
3. **Time Management Extensions**:
   - ○ **StayFocusd**: A productivity extension that helps you stay focused by limiting the time spent on distracting websites.
   - ○ **Toggl Track**: A time tracking extension that integrates with Google Workspace apps to log time spent on various tasks.

💡 *Tip: Explore the Chrome Web Store for a wide variety of extensions that suit your productivity needs and integrate seamlessly with Google Workspace.*

Conclusion

Integrating Google Workspace with third-party apps like Zapier, Slack, Trello, and Asana, along with utilizing productivity-boosting Chrome extensions, can significantly enhance your workflow and team collaboration. These integrations automate tasks, streamline communication, and allow you to focus on more important work. Take advantage of these powerful tools to create a more efficient and organized work environment.

PART SEVEN

Troubleshooting & Expert Tips

Chapter Eighteen

Troubleshooting Common Google Workspace Issues

E ven though Google Workspace offers a powerful suite of tools, users may occasionally encounter problems or technical hiccups. This chapter provides practical solutions for some of the most common issues faced by Google Workspace users, including recovering lost files, resolving syncing issues, and troubleshooting Google Meet connectivity problems.

Recovering Lost Files & Restoring Deleted Emails

1. **Recovering Lost Files in Google Drive**:
   - **Accidentally Deleted Files**: If you've mistakenly deleted files from Google Drive, don't panic! Google Drive offers a **trash bin** where deleted files are temporarily stored before being permanently erased.
     - **How to Recover**:
       1. Open Google Drive.
       2. Click on "Trash" in the left-hand menu.
       3. Find the file you want to restore, right-click on it, and select **Restore**.
   - **Google Drive Version History**: If you need to revert to a previous version of a file:

1. Right-click on the file in Google Drive and select **Manage Versions**.
2. Choose the version you want to restore and click **Download** or **Restore**.

- ○ **File Recovery Beyond Trash**: If you've emptied your trash or cannot find the file, you can request a file recovery from Google support. Files are recoverable up to 25 days after they've been deleted permanently.

2. **Restoring Deleted Emails in Gmail**:
   - ○ **Email Trash**: Gmail temporarily stores deleted emails in the **Trash** for 30 days before they are permanently deleted.
     - ▪ **How to Recover**:
       1. Open Gmail and go to the **Trash** folder.
       2. Find the email you want to recover and click **Move to Inbox** or drag it to another folder.
   - ○ **Recovering Emails After 30 Days**: If the email is no longer in the Trash, use the Gmail support tool to request email recovery.
     - ▪ **How to Request Recovery**:
       1. Go to the **Gmail Help Center**.
       2. Click on **Contact Us** and select **Missing Email** to initiate a recovery request.

💡 *Tip: Regularly back up important files and emails to avoid losing them due to accidental deletions.*

Fixing Sync Issues with Google Drive & Calendar

1. **Google Drive Sync Issues**:
   - ○ **Check Google Drive Storage**: If your Google Drive isn't syncing, ensure you have enough available storage. If your storage is full, you can't upload new files or sync existing ones.
     - ▪ **How to Check Storage**:

1. Go to **Google Drive** and click on the gear icon (settings).
2. Under **Storage**, check your current usage. You can upgrade your storage or delete unwanted files.

- o **Force Sync on Google Drive**:
    1. On the desktop, ensure **Google Drive for Desktop** is running.
    2. Right-click on the Google Drive icon in your taskbar/system tray and select **Sync now**.
- o **Clear Cache and Cookies**: Sometimes, clearing your browser's cache and cookies can resolve sync issues.
    - **How to Clear Cache**:
        1. Go to your browser's settings.
        2. Find **Privacy and Security**, then select **Clear browsing data**.
        3. Choose **Cookies and Cached Images** and click **Clear Data**.

2. **Google Calendar Sync Issues**:
   - o **Check Calendar Sync Settings**: Make sure your Google Calendar is syncing properly on both desktop and mobile devices. If you've recently updated your app or system, syncing may be disrupted.
       - **Mobile App Sync**:
           1. Open **Google Calendar** on your mobile device.
           2. Go to **Settings** and ensure the calendar is syncing. Toggle it off and on again to refresh.
       - **Desktop Sync**:
           - Go to **Google Calendar**, check if the calendar is syncing by refreshing the page.
   - o **Conflicting Time Zones**: Ensure that your calendar events are set to the correct time zone to avoid sync issues, especially when dealing with multiple time zones.

💡 *Tip: Sync issues can often be resolved by simply disconnecting and reconnecting your Google account or app on the affected device.*

Resolving Google Meet Connectivity Issues

Google Meet is a popular tool for video conferencing, but connectivity issues can sometimes disrupt meetings. Here's how to troubleshoot and resolve common problems.

1. **Check Your Internet Connection**:
   - **Weak Wi-Fi**: Poor internet connection is one of the most common causes of Google Meet connectivity issues. Try moving closer to your router or switching to a wired connection.
   - **Speed Test**: Ensure that your internet connection meets the minimum required speed for video conferencing.
     - **Minimum Speed**: Google recommends a minimum of 3.2 Mbps download and upload speeds for HD video calls.
2. **Clear Your Browser Cache**:
   - **Cache Issues**: A buildup of cached data in your browser can affect the performance of Google Meet. Clearing your browser's cache may resolve the issue.
     - **How to Clear Cache**: Go to your browser settings, find the **Privacy & Security** section, and clear your cache and cookies.
3. **Update Your Browser & Google Meet App**:
   - **Outdated Version**: Ensure that your browser or the Google Meet app is up to date. Sometimes, older versions may cause issues with connectivity.
     - **Update Browser**: Check for updates in the browser settings and update it to the latest version.
     - **Update Google Meet App**: If using the app on mobile, visit your app store and check for updates.
4. **Disable Browser Extensions**:
   - **Conflicting Extensions**: Some browser extensions can interfere with Google Meet, leading to issues like frozen screens or audio

problems. Try disabling any unnecessary extensions to see if that resolves the problem.

- **How to Disable Extensions**: Go to your browser settings and manage the extensions.

5. **Grant Permissions to Google Meet**:
   - **Microphone & Camera Access**: Ensure that your browser or app has permission to access your microphone and camera. Without proper permissions, Google Meet won't work properly.
     - **Check Permissions**: Go to your browser settings, find the **Permissions** section, and allow access to the camera and microphone for Google Meet.

💡 *Tip: Before joining a meeting, use the Google Meet "Check Your Settings" feature to ensure everything is set up correctly, including video and audio options.*

Conclusion

While Google Workspace is an incredibly reliable platform, issues can arise from time to time. By following the solutions provided in this chapter, you can quickly resolve common problems, like recovering lost files, fixing syncing issues, and troubleshooting Google Meet connectivity. Regular maintenance and staying updated with the latest software versions can help prevent many of these issues in the future.

If problems persist despite following these steps, don't hesitate to reach out to Google support for further assistance.

Chapter Nineteen

Pro Tips & Hidden Gems in Google Workspace

G oogle Workspace is packed with hidden features and tools that can help you work more efficiently and make the most of its extensive suite of tools. In this chapter, we'll dive into must-know keyboard shortcuts, free resources, and the latest updates to Google Workspace that will boost your productivity and make your workspace smarter.

Must-Know Keyboard Shortcuts for Faster Work

Keyboard shortcuts are a game-changer when it comes to speeding up your workflow. They can help you navigate Google Workspace tools faster, manage tasks with ease, and get more done in less time. Here are some of the top shortcuts you should use regularly:

1. **Google Docs Shortcuts**:
    o **Bold Text**: Ctrl + B (Windows) / Cmd + B (Mac)
    o **Italicize Text**: Ctrl + I (Windows) / Cmd + I (Mac)
    o **Strikethrough Text**: Alt + Shift + 5 (Windows) / Cmd + Shift + X (Mac)
    o **Insert Hyperlink**: Ctrl + K (Windows) / Cmd + K (Mac)
2. **Google Sheets Shortcuts**:

- o **Insert New Row**: Shift + Space (to select row), then Ctrl + Shift + + (Windows) / Cmd + Shift + + (Mac)
- o **Fill Cell with Formula**: Ctrl + Enter (Windows) / Cmd + Enter (Mac)
- o **Navigate Between Sheets**: Ctrl + Page Up/Page Down (Windows) / Cmd + Page Up/Page Down (Mac)

3. **Google Drive Shortcuts**:
   - o **Open Google Drive Search**: / (Windows & Mac)
   - o **Create New Document**: Shift + T (Windows & Mac)
   - o **Share File**: Ctrl + Alt + S (Windows) / Cmd + Alt + S (Mac)

4. **Google Calendar Shortcuts**:
   - o **Create New Event**: C (Windows & Mac)
   - o **Go to Today's Date**: T (Windows & Mac)
   - o **Navigate Between Views**: 1 for Day view, 2 for Week view, 3 for Month view

💡 *Tip: Keep a list of your most-used shortcuts handy to master them more quickly and reduce your reliance on the mouse.*

Free Google Workspace Resources & Templates

Google Workspace offers a wealth of free resources and templates that can help you get started quickly, stay organized, and improve your productivity. These tools can save you time and effort, allowing you to focus on the task at hand.

1. **Google Workspace Templates**:
   - o **Google Docs**: Choose from a wide selection of **resume templates**, **reports**, **letters**, and more.
     - Access them via: Google Docs > Template Gallery.
   - o **Google Sheets**: Find templates for **budget tracking**, **project management**, and **data analysis**.
     - Access them via: Google Sheets > Template Gallery.
   - o **Google Slides**: Use **presentation templates** designed for a variety of needs, from business meetings to creative projects.

- Access them via: Google Slides > Template Gallery.
  - o **Google Forms**: Create surveys, quizzes, and questionnaires quickly using free templates.
    - Access them via: Google Forms > Template Gallery.
2. **Google Workspace Learning Resources**:
   - o **Google Help Center**: Access guides, FAQs, and troubleshooting tips for all Google Workspace apps.
     - Visit: [Google Help Center](#).
   - o **Google Workspace Training**: Google offers free online courses and certification for Workspace users. Enhance your skills and learn best practices with Google's official training materials.
     - Visit: Google Workspace Training.
3. **Google Workspace Marketplace**:
   - o Discover third-party integrations to enhance your experience. Whether you're looking for project management tools, document signing apps, or automation solutions, the Marketplace offers plenty of options.

💡 *Tip: Using Google's pre-designed templates will save you time and make your projects look more professional with minimal effort.*

Latest Google Workspace Updates & Features

Google is always rolling out new updates and features to improve the usability and functionality of Google Workspace tools. Staying up to date with these changes will help you make the most out of the platform. Here are some of the latest Google Workspace updates you should know about:

1. **Smart Compose & Smart Reply (Gmail & Google Docs)**:
   - o **Smart Compose** in Gmail helps you write emails faster by suggesting text based on your writing style.
   - o **Smart Reply** offers quick, context-aware responses to emails, saving you time on routine responses.

- These features are now available in both Gmail and Google Docs, enhancing your writing process with AI-driven suggestions.

2. **Google Meet Updates**:
   - **Live Captions**: Google Meet now offers live captions during video calls in various languages, helping to improve accessibility and comprehension.
   - **Enhanced Security Features**: You can now lock your Google Meet room before starting the meeting to prevent uninvited participants from joining.

3. **Google Drive Improvements**:
   - **Offline Mode for Google Docs, Sheets, and Slides**: You can now access and edit your documents even when you're offline, with changes syncing automatically when you reconnect.
   - **Improved File Sharing**: Google Drive now lets you share files with multiple people at once, with enhanced privacy controls.

4. **Google Calendar & Google Tasks Enhancements**:
   - **Multiple Time Zone Support**: Google Calendar now supports multiple time zones for events, making it easier to schedule across different regions.
   - **Task Integration with Google Calendar**: Tasks from Google Tasks can now be added directly to your calendar, helping you stay organized and on top of your to-dos.

5. **Google Workspace Admin Console Features**:
   - **Advanced Reporting Tools**: Admins can now access detailed activity reports for all Workspace apps, allowing for better monitoring and security.
   - **Improved User Management**: Admins have more control over permissions and can now delegate tasks with greater flexibility.

💡 *Tip: Enable automatic updates for your Google Workspace apps so that you can take advantage of the newest features without having to manually update.*

Conclusion

Mastering Google Workspace means knowing how to leverage keyboard shortcuts, utilize free resources and templates, and stay updated on the latest features. By integrating these expert tips and hidden gems into your daily routine, you'll be able to maximize your productivity and get the most out of Google Workspace's vast toolset.

Index

www.ingramcontent.com/pod-product-compliance
Lightning Source LLC
LaVergne TN
LVHW081527050326
832903LV00025B/1658